MURDER AND DIFFERENCE

Indiana Studies in Biblical Literature

Herbert Marks and Robert Polzin,
General Editors

MURDER AND DIFFERENCE

Gender, Genre, and Scholarship
on Sisera's Death

MIEKE
BAL

Translated by Matthew Gumpert

INDIANA UNIVERSITY PRESS
BLOOMINGTON & INDIANAPOLIS

For Daan Hoogland

Manufactured in the United States of America

Library of Congress Cataloging-in-Publication Data

Bal, Mieke, 1946–
Murder and difference.

(Indiana studies in biblical literature)
Bibliography: p.
Includes index.
1. Bible. O.T. Judges IV–V—Criticism,
interpretation, etc.   2. Sisera (Biblical figure)
3. Jael (Biblical figure)   4. Deborah (Biblical judge)
I. Title.   II. Series.
BS1305.2.B35   1987   222'.3206   86-42995
ISBN 0-253-33905-7

1 2 3 4 5 91 90 89 88 87

CONTENTS

But why should all the implications suggested by language be consistent?

Walter Ong

i vitelli dei romani sono belli:
—go, Vitellius, to the sound of war of the Roman god
—the calves of the Romans are beautiful

Umberto Eco

Judgment is cognition, functioning as an act. . . . Judging is nothing less than the wielding of power over life and death through language.

Barbara Johnson

PREFACE

"To criticize," in the etymological sense, means /to differentiate/. Today the verb designates a socially relevant practice that seeks to denounce ideologies considered dangerous. It is the concern of the present study to show that these two meanings are in fact one and the same; for the pernicious character of certain ideologies lies in a centripetal force that stimulates uniformity and the subordination of groups and subgroups to the dominant group. Consequently, the will to differentiate necessarily enters into any critical practice in the current sense.

The key concept in this study is that of *code*. I will use the term to designate those aspects of the signifying practice which semiotic theory acknowledges but whose consequences it has not sufficiently addressed. Regarded as a rule of correlation between expression and content, the code will be studied in its relation to the *conventions* that found it, the *plurality* that characterizes it, the *materiality* that makes it culturally accessible, the *constraints* that control its activity, and the *institutions* that are its natural setting. All of these will be analyzed with regard to their consequences for the cultural practice that is *the treatment of a semiotic object*.

Once I had established the aim of this project—the analysis of the relation between the concept of code and critical practice as differentiation—it was necessary to decide upon a specific object of study. The most appropriate choice seemed to me that of a plural object, treated in varying degrees as unified: two versions of the narration of a spectacular event. The texts in question being part of the Hebrew Bible, they are at once historically "distant," which in itself imposes a diachronic perspective, and very actively present in our culture, which allows us, in still another way, to differentiate.

In order to limit the material, I considered, among the innumerable codes applicable to this case, those which are anchored in the institution of the university so as to form a relatively homogeneous and representative group. The following premise will be our starting point: that the hermeneutic approach practiced within an academic field or discipline is based on a code that defines and delineates this field or discipline.

This enterprise is both more limited and broader in scope than the one that Saïd conducted in his *Orientalism*, or Todorov in his *La Découverte de l'Amérique*. Like them, I will attempt to follow the kinds of reasoning that conceal ethnocentrism and androcentrism. Saïd and Todorov study a particular prejudice enunciated in relation to various texts; I will address different prejudices enunciated in regard to the same two succinct fragments. Moreover, I will restrict the analysis to the interpretive practice and its interaction with other activities of research. My conclusions will bear uniquely upon the differential capacity of codes. In contrast to Saïd and Todorov, I will be led to submit possible interpretive beginnings in the hope of showing that criticism of the way codes are used should not lead to the condemnation of the codes themselves, which would leave interpreters powerless.

The final destination of the path that lies before us is the proposal of an interpretive approach that combines, in a rational and disciplined manner, the contributions of several codes, any one of which, taken by itself, would be too unifying. Progressing along that path will be then, an experience of interdisciplinarity; we will discover the importance, the urgency of that approach by way of the limits of the disciplinary discourse, whose inadequacy will become progressively manifest as we proceed. If the discipline is constantly challenged, it is not with the intention of utterly discrediting it, but rather to demonstrate to what degree the semiotic aspect inherent in every scientific activity influences, or even determines, results that would gain in interest if their orientations and biases were more openly weighed. On the other hand, the critical power of the codes will be measured by their capacity to differentiate the two fragments under consideration. From this differentiation to a truly critical practice, there is only a step: one that hermeneutics alone cannot make but for which it can provide the proper foundations.

The primary inspiration for this book came from the intersemiotic seminar at the Université du Québec à Montréal, where a first draft was submitted to an alert and stimulating audience. It has been elaborated as the result of discussions with Fokkelien van Dijk and others. Ernst van Alphen helped with constant constructive criticism and encouragement. Its final form owes very much to Ria and Ton Lemaire, who provided not only feedback, information, and suggestions, but also the stimulating environment of their home.

The English version has been carefully prepared by Matthew Gumpert. I am grateful for his efforts and patience, which have led to the best possible result. I was able to put the finishing touches on the book during my year at the Harvard Divinity School, where I was invited by the Women's Studies in Religion Program.

I dedicate this book to my son, as another way of speaking to him, for the understanding and acceptance of difference.

THE OBJECT

24. Blessed above [the] women be Jael,
woman of Heber the Kenite
blessed among [the] women in the tent.

25. He asked for water
she gave him milk
in a lordly bowl she brought forth cream.

26. Her hand she stretched out to the tent peg
and her right hand to the workmen's hammer
and she pounded Sisera, she crushed his head
and she shattered and pierced his temple.

27. Between her feet he collapsed, he fell, he lay still
between her feet he collapsed, he fell,
where he collapsed, he fell, undone/overcome.

28. At the window she looked out and cried,
through the lattice, the mother of Sisera,
why is his chariot so slow to come
why do the hoofbeats of his chariot delay?

29. The wisest of her princesses answered,
nay, to herself she answered:

30. Are they not finding and dividing the spoil,
one womb/girl, two wombs/girls for each hero's head,
spoil of dyed cloth for Sisera,
spoil of dyed cloth embroidered,
dyed cloth twice embroidered for his neck?

JUDGES 4:

18. And Jael went out to meet Sisera and said to him: turn in, my lord,
turn in to me. Fear not. And he turned in to her into the tent and
she covered him with a curtain.

19. And he said to her: give me a little water to drink for I am
thirsty, and she opened a skin of milk and gave him some to drink and
she covered him.

20. And he said to her: stand at the door of the tent and if a man
comes and asks you and says: is there a man here? then say: no.

21. And Jael woman of Heber took a tent peg and seized the hammer in her hand and she went to him softly and she drove the peg into his temple, and it penetrated into the earth, and he was fast asleep and he was weary and he died.

22. And behold, Barak pursuing Sisera, and Jael came out to meet him and said to him: come, and I will show you the man you seek. And he came in to her and behold: Sisera fallen, dead and the peg in his temple.

INTRODUCTION

The most widely read commentaries on the book of Judges generally concur in fixing the date of the book's composition at the seventh century. Its most ancient sections are dated somewhere around 980 B.C., with the exception of chapter 5, the victorious hymn of Deborah, which is assumed to be contemporaneous with the event about which she sings. According to Cundall (1968:34) and Albright (1968:117–18), that event must have occurred somewhere around 1125 B.C. Between the texts of chapters 4 and 5, there is thus a difference of a hundred years. The adventures Deborah sings about could represent a first phase in the conquest—mythic or real, it doesn't much matter here—of Palestine. At the time of this war, "Israel" was the deceptively unifying name of a number of tribes dispersed throughout a territory inhabited by other peoples. Judges seems, indeed, to describe the painful process of the development of a "national" unity, something that will not be fully accomplished, and even then without stability, for at least another hundred years. During this period of transition, the tribes were assimilated by urban and agrarian peoples who spoke other languages, had other customs, and venerated other gods.

If it seems at first glance an exaggeration to suppose that the Hebrew of the book in its entirety and that of chapter 5 differ as profoundly as the Latin and Italian of the fragment cited in the epigraph, it should be pointed out that translators and philologists have despaired over the text of the song of Deborah, which is so archaic that "In as many as seventy percent of the verses the meaning of a key word is doubtful" (Auld 1984:157). It seems to me to be good practice, if we want to escape falling into the universalist perspective, to assume the probability of profound changes of all kinds, and, consequently, to historicize the investigation and the interpretation. Chapter 4 narrates the same event that is the inspiration for chapter 5, the enthusiastic song of the prophetess, poetess, judge, and military leader, Deborah. The two versions differ, which is hardly surprising, and the list of differences has long been established. They are situated at three levels: that of politics (who is the Canaanite chief, Jabin or Sisera?), of geography (where did the tribes who participated in the combat come from, and how is it possible that

1

they were reunited without the knowledge of the enemy?), and of tribal association (which tribes participated?). Now and then a theological difference is also noticed; the image of Yahweh is different in the two versions. In 4, he is the god of war; in 5, he is a deity of cosmic proportions, and his military aspect is derived from this vision. As for the differences between the two descriptions of the murder of Sisera, they seem striking to me; Cundall, however, considers them minor ("slight dissimilarities") and attributable to the incomplete character of the document (92). I cannot help but wonder why linguistic and historical differences were enhanced only to minimize the more basic differences. I would situate the latter at an intermediate level, that of representation: the focalization, the choice of details, the literary form. As for the "crucial" scene of the murder, the most glaring differences could well be represented as diegetic disproportions; each version gives both "too much" and "too little" with respect to the other. The eulogy addressed to Jael in chapter 5 and the stanza concerning Sisera's mother, which follows the description of the murder, are both absent from chapter 4; in the more recent version, verse 20, Sisera gives instructions to Jael: this element is missing from chapter 5. Besides these massive differences, there are differences of emphasis, which fall under the heading "slight dissimilarities"; for example, the repeated mention of the name of Jael's "husband" in chapter 4, the mention of the cream added in chapter 5 (probably this refers to "curds," a thick yogurt), and the description of Sisera's death, detailed in 5, assigned a causal motivation in 4.

Woman's song—man's epic? The conclusion is plausible that Deborah is either the real or the fictional author of the song, the enunciator of the lyric discourse. But the assessment of gender is in itself only of limited interest. I intend to examine in greater detail the question raised by the differences between the two versions of the murder of Sisera, in a systematic confrontation of the two texts and the different disciplines that have tried to interpret them. My starting point will be the concept of *code* as it is currently accepted in semiotics. The four disciplines under consideration—history, theology, anthropology, and literary analysis—will be envisioned in the way they function as code: as a rule of correlation institutionally tied to a group that projects its own interests upon it. The contribution of each method will be considered primarily as the result of the semiotic functioning of the discipline. Our interest will lie in the potential of these methods for the interpretation of differences as such, and, on the other hand, in the different kinds of blindness (ranging from defective vision to the stubborn refusal to see) that prevent them from furthering this interpretation.

The almost exclusive emphasis on the *interpretation* of *differences* was determined by methodological considerations. Disregarding whatever differences of method may separate the sciences, I begin with the premise that every scientific effort includes, to some degree, a factor of interpretation. In contrast to a causal explanation *strictu sensu*, a hermeneutical explanation—in the general, not the theological sense (see Ricoeur 1984:321)—seeks to illuminate the differences between rather than the laws common to phenomena. This feature is what makes hermeneutics relevant to this study. The explanation of the phenomenon in question, the difference between two texts of disparate origin, raises the problem of two kinds of explanation and their interrelations. Any discipline that attempts to choose rigorously between explanation and interpretation, while opening the way to certain aspects, closes off others, and thus is likely to thwart its own contribution. To proscribe interpretation and differences is to refuse to see the characteristics of the code that a discipline implies. The activity of interpretation extends the limits of the discipline itself, inasmuch as it gives access to other semiotic practices. Hermeneutics and interdisciplinarity go hand in hand.

If disciplinary codes are by definition limiting, this drawback does not mean that what I call the transdisciplinary codes—those which are not integrated within a determined discipline but which, having a certain autonomy outside the institution and often perceived as "fact," something "obvious," are easily accepted—are necessarily more open and more effective in facing differences. After the consideration of four disciplinary codes, the *thematic* code, which is transdisciplinary, will be confronted with the *gender code;** the latter, equally transdisciplinary, will be used by virtue of its own presuppositions to transfer the interpretation to other, disciplinary codes. The result of this examination will be a plea for the *interdisciplinary* code, which, although open, will not be eclectic but *disciplined* to the extent that it recognizes itself as a code, with all a code's limitations, interests, and hermeneutic power.

In elucidating the interpretative process we gain nothing dwelling on the definition of a code, or on the precise limits of the term. I accept its current sense, as adopted by Eco (1976, 1984); I am interested only in its methodological implications and critical possibilities. Among its characteristics I retain the following:

1. *Codes are conventional.* "There is a signification system (and therefore a code) when there is the socially conventionalized possibility of generating sign functions . . ." (Eco 1976:4). This social aspect carries with it two implications for the present study: on the one hand it leads to a certain sectarianism (one group excludes another); on the other, contrary to the universalist perspective, it creates of necessity an open

---

*The *gender code* is a code based on gender differentiation, on the distinction between the sexes; it is "le code sexué."—TRANS.

system with possibilities of access to diverse points of view: the group itself is not a closed system but is divided into subgroups, which are themselves further divided, and is regrouped into larger units. In addition, it is historically variable.

2. *Codes are plural.* "What was called 'the code' is thus better viewed as *a complex network of subcodes* . . ." (Eco 1976:125). It is not only the plurality of groups in which the codes are anchored that necessarily results in a plurality of codes; each subgroup brings its codes, and each member of the group is also a member of one or more subgroups and larger groups. The codes are also subordinate to the hypercode; this condition ensures that in different situations of enunciation or of nonverbal signification, combinations of specific codes apply, like the codes of genres, the cognitive codes, legal codes, affective codes; most of the time all of these are at work, because situations of signification are themselves "mixed."

3. *Codes are correlative.* "Every item in the code maintains a double set of relations, a *systematic* one with all the items of its own plane (content or expression) and a *signifying* one with one or more items from the correlated plane" (Eco 1976:126). If Eco is right, the distinction he establishes elsewhere between codes of expression and codes of content (which he prefers to call subcodes) is void. It is true that there are two *systems* correlated; however, one of two things must be true: either the systematic relations within a level—for example, relations of opposition—are already signifying, hence correlative, or they constitute part of a code but are not themselves one. We need only compare Lacan's concept of the "chain of signifiers" with Peirce's concept of the interpretant to see that intrasystemic relations are already virtually correlative because the two levels distinguished are separable only in theory, and cease to be as soon as signification enters into the picture.

4. *Codes are material.* " . . . the industrialization of communications changes not only the conditions for receiving and sending out messages but . . . the very meaning of the message" (Eco 1976:13). This idea is even more obvious when one studies the consequences that the evolution of writing out of an originally oral culture has had for thought, language, and cultural expression in general. Ong (1977, 1982) and Goody and Watt (1968) in anthropological studies, and Zumthor (1982) in a literary study, offer convincing views of the functional differences between the two systems of signification. Not only the structures of messages but even their meanings are affected.

5. *Codes are restrictive.* This feature is a consequence of the conventional character of codes. On the other hand, as codes are not stable and because historical changes are swift and ineluctable, a consideration of those changes makes it possible for us to analyze the restrictions

and constraints in this dynamism itself. It is when *difference* is suspended that restriction is apparent. The restrictive character of codes leaves itself open to criticism from two related but different angles. Thus we have the following characteristics:

6. *Codes are interested.* Because codes are anchored in social life, and specifically in that of a particular group, they are inevitably biased by the interests of that group. This aspect of semiosis as social practice has been analyzed by Habermas (1968; see Bal, 1986). Bias determined by and serving an interest exerts, along with the restrictions inherent in the functioning of codes, a real cultural power. The groups in power have the power over signs. They *possess* the codes; they determine which meanings are permitted and which meanings are prohibited, according to the interests that are served by this legislation. Since groups are heterogeneous, these "laws over rules" or metarules are not stable, and still less transhistorical; they are subordinated to that centripetal tendency which goes hand in hand with power itself, and which it is our purpose here to bring to light and criticize.

7. *Codes are institutionalized.* This characteristic is correlative to the others. If not, there would be perfect agreement between social groups, their interests, and the language they employ. How to explain, then, that those in power are obliged to employ all possible means to affirm and reaffirm their grip on the codes they control? It is true that today the school is the preeminent institution where the codes acceptable to the dominant group are separated from those deemed unacceptable, whether the latter belong to particular classes, dialects, age groups, or genders (Rose 1984). But the school's task proves to be a difficult one, and although the institution may indeed lead a less troubled existence than subgroups or the individual, the fact remains that, to give an example, teenagers who see one another only in class speak a language that adults uninformed of the code, including the representatives of the institution, do not understand. I will proceed from the idea, then, that there is a connection between codes and institutions, a fragile and variable, but also centripetal, link. Codes that are systematically fought by institutions, be they schools, churches, states, or others, are in danger of disappearing, for the sanctions of institutions are extremely prohibitive. However, within the margins of *difference*, codes are tenacious.

These are the characteristics of the code that I intend to explore in this study of the two versions of the story of Jael's ambiguous act. But why, I hear someone protest, make use of this concept rather than another, for example, *ideology*, or *the unconscious*, or *positions of power, semantic field*, or *narrative scenario*, or what have you? Because the concept of code, especially if it is understood with the particular emphases I have lent it, allows all these other notions to be joined, and to be integrated within the social mechanism of language. It is broad enough to include, and hence to integrate, aspects different from but related to those I have enumerated. After the feeling of dissatisfaction that the vigorous and important efforts of disciplines like semantics, narratology, and logic left us with (an effect due, I believe, to the atomization and the abstraction of the object that they imposed), the prospect of such an integration is attractive. The concept of code can be integrated within the comprehensive perspective of cultural anthropology, which attempts, in turn, to integrate the different aspects of the cultural process into an all-embracing theory. The concept of code, which is semiotic, is easily related to that of *theme*, which is semantic; the first describes how the second functions.

It is partly this synthetic perspective that makes the code such a powerful critical concept. It enables us to see how it functions, this "vie des signes au sein de la vie sociale" (life of signs within social life) that de Saussure wanted to study. The power of the code is also a function of its specificity. The conventional character of codes makes it possible to see how groups structure themselves into a pluralistic linguistic community, and to what extent groups and subgroups, through the use of different codes for the encoding and decoding of the same expressions or the same contents, enter into disagreements. Moreover, the natural plurality of codes shows us that language functions in different ways *at the same time,* and *never,* for example, purely according to the conversational maxims of Grice (1976). The network is a more appropriate metaphor than the hierarchy. A network is by definition structured without being ordered in hierarchical form. I will insist upon this characteristic.

The correlative character of codes leads to the axiom of the omnipresence of meaning, since there are correlations everywhere. This axiom neutralizes the prescriptive and restrictive character of codes, their tendency toward universality. It opens up the mind: we see multiple possibilities in the interpretation of texts that are culturally distant in time and/or space as well as in the production of new meanings in today's emerging subcultures. It is an axiom that makes us alert to the jurisdiction of meaning in social life, even in those situations where we assume we are dealing merely with "facts," with "necessities," with "what is natural." The centripetal force of the codes becomes apparent on the semantic plane through *thematization.* The tendency toward semantic unity brings about a progressive reification of recurrent meanings. Hermeneutics must analyze this process while compensating for it by a sustained attention to differences, a desire to be centrifugal.

An awareness of the material anchoring of codes can guard against cultural ethnocentrism, which would prevent us from seeing meaning in cultural differences or in the semiotic practices of different subgroups within our own culture. We would see nothing there but a lack, a preceding stage, primitive or underdeveloped. The characteristics of restriction, interest, and institutionalization, finally, are obviously crucial for a critical analysis of cultural objects. Codes control interpretation; they are assisted in this by institutions, which propagate certain codes while discrediting or silencing others. It emerges clearly from the reception of our object of study that this bias is taken seriously, as a cultural necessity.

Focusing a little more closely upon the problematics facing us, I would like to return to one of the first examples of signification that Eco (1976) presents. He is discussing unintentional signs, that is, symptoms. The phenomenon of the symptom has great significance for the discussion of cultures different from ours, since the knowledge of intention, presupposed in the *signal,* is irreparably out of reach. At the same time Eco's example offers the advantage of thematizing cultural plurality.

> Even if we do not know the socialized meanings of those gestures we can at any rate recognize the gesturer as Italian, Jew, Anglo-Saxon and so on, just as almost everybody is able to recognize a Chinese or a German speaker as such even if he does not know Chinese or German. These behaviors are able to signify even though the sender does not attribute such a capacity to them. (Eco 1976:18)

The example is fascinating because it supplies, undoubtedly in spite of Eco's intentions, *a semiotic description of racism,* and of other practices of discrimination, like ethnocentrism and sexism. It is the ever-widening gap between the intention of the sender, who is not, in principle, concerned with his/her own identity as the *other,* and the insufficient knowledge from which the interpreter of the sender's codes suffers, that creates the void in which the racist code can implant itself. The example demonstrates in fact to what extent codes are necessarily correlative: meaning comes to occupy all empty space, emptiness being the most frightening sign of what is different, and ignorance of codes cancels all other signification save that already known by the interpreter. I would have been happier if Eco, just to demonstrate his critical goodwill, had taken his analysis further and stated more precisely that the capacity to *recognize* a Chinese as Chinese is based on the addressee's choice to attribute this particular sense to non-sense. Even without raising the question of how to know which part of this interpretive act is really based on the gestures, the intonation, etc., of the sender, and which, on the other hand, is simply founded on physical appearance, which is also considered significant, Eco could have clarified what happens during this "symptomatic" practice. The potential connotation /other/ becomes denotation here, because all other denotations are out of reach. The less familiar the denotative codes of a culture, the more urgent this inversion becomes, imposed by the ever-expanding semantic void. In contrast, the

more the interpreter becomes aware of codes that were previously unknown to her/him, the more narrow the void is, and hence the less
urgent the need will be to latch onto the most obvious aspect in order to
graft a superficial meaning upon it.

The example illustrates how important the knowledge of codes is for
obtaining access to texts that are distant from us in space or time. In the
case of Judges 4 and 5, the problem is exemplary: the linguistic code of
the song is in great measure lost, which leaves the philologists empty-
handed. What to do? The lost code is replaced by other codes, belonging
to various interpretive practices: historical, theological, anthropological,
and literary. These interpretive codes, which I refer to as such because
they proceed from the modern reader and not from the addressee fore-
seen by the sender, are all put to work in attempts to retrieve or at least
approach the lost codes. In other words, they are all motivated by the
same desire: to overcome the attitude described by Eco; the text is therefore acknowledged to be inaccessible even while it is interpreted. I will
illustrate a number of these interpretive practices by giving examples of
the codes commonly used in biblical interpretation. Two codes frequently applied, the philological and the moral code, will not be treated in and
of themselves.

The *philological* code, which has yielded more or less biased translations, is treated here as a preliminary subcode, appealed to at moments
of need by the codes under consideration. Operating in an objectivist
spirit of scientific rigor, philology is an indispensable tool, which does not
imply that it is disinterested or exempt from bias. I am considering it
here only as accessory simply because it does not form part of any synthetic effort. It studies each particular word that raises a problem, each
line that is difficult to decode, without seeking to interpret the text as a
whole.

The second code excluded from the main focus of our study is the
moral code. Despite its extraordinary power, this code is discounted because it is inevitably anachronistic and is not characterized by an effort to
rejoin the codes of the text. It is also parasitic: we will see just how
difficult it is for the interpreters to avoid this tendency. If philology is
situated within the interpretive effort whose foundations it provides, the
moral code is situated beyond or parallel to this effort, even while sometimes claiming to be above it. It tends to arrogate meanings brought to
light by means of other codes, without fearing incoherence, universal-
ism, or anachronism, and it will often be necessary to point out its insin-
uation into the disciplinary discourses. While the philological code does
not lead to the interpretation of a thematic network, the moral code
imposes a unified and preestablished theme upon every signifying element. While philology can be seen as an enterprise of overcoding (Eco
1976:136: "Thus overcoding proceeds from existing codes to more ana-

lytic codes"), the moral code is something closer to an undercoding procedure (Eco 1976:135–36: "Undercoding may be defined as the opera-
tion by means of which in the absence of reliable pre-established rules,
certain macroscopic portions of certain texts are provisionally assumed
to be pertinent units of a code in formation"). Neither of these two codes
can be ignored, but they do not have an autonomous place in the discussion that follows.

I chose two kinds of examples for my study. The first category consists
of research that the specialists, citing frequently from it, have recognized
as valuable. This is a body of interpretations that, although necessarily
biased, are manifestly honest and strive not to be anachronistic. All of
them seek the impossible contemporaneity with the object they address,
the *coevality* that we must pursue despite its impossibility (see Fabian
1983). The second category consists of works of popularization. I pro-
ceeded in the following manner. First I consulted lay commentaries,
available to the public in ordinary bookstores. In these texts, the results
of disciplinary studies have been "translated" in order to provide believers interested in the Bible with interpretive directions. At least this is
supposed to be what happens. We know how often the process is reversed, that is, how often popular views implicitly inform the results of
scholarly efforts. Next, I consulted more academic sources from the
same discipline on which the popular commentaries were based. This
procedure greatly limited my choice of examples, there being certain
kinds of research that lend themselves more to popularization, and others less so. The clearest example is the historical code: among the many
subdisciplines of history it is, on the one hand, the historical criticism of
texts and, on the other, the study of collective history and politics whose
results are most often retained in popular commentaries.

The choice, therefore, was determined by the degree of acceptance of
disciplinary codes. This factor allows us to grasp as clearly as possible the
intercultural communication that the codes establish.

The goal of this demonstration is threefold:

1. It will prove possible to integrate the different meanings that result,
   thereby demonstrating the *a priori* plurality of the signifying practice.
   The different semantic lines, the isotopies that lead to *themes*, are at
   the same time clearly distinct and perfectly compatible.
2. The codes lead us, I will show, far into the understanding of the text
   and its cultural background, but *at the same time* they reveal to what
   degree their bias imposes, stimulates, or permits a practice of censorship that stems from the restriction and the institutionalization of
   codes.
3. The codes in question, despite sometimes important results, are incapable of interpreting the striking differences between the two repre-

sentations of the death of Sisera. An interpretive leap or undercoded *abduction* (Eco 1984:42) becomes indispensable. This type of abduction consists in selecting a rule (a code) among a series of alternatives all equally possible. Eco states more precisely: "the decision as to whether certain properties (belonging to the meaning of the term) must be blown up or narcotized represents a good case of undercoded abduction."

In our case, this interpretive leap will appear in two forms. One consists in following a code that I will call *thematic*. It distinguishes itself from the preceding codes by its transdisciplinary character. In other words, it refuses to be limited *a priori* by any specific discipline. Nor does it demand the aid of disciplinary codes, as would an interdisciplinary code. A second feature characteristic of the thematic code is the presupposition of the semantic unity of the text. The abductive aspect lies in the *a priori*—and in principle entirely undetermined—choice of a theme that is not prescribed by any discipline. This code, too, is incapable of resolving all the problems. Free relative to specific academic institutions, it is biased by the same horror of contradiction and difference that characterizes the confirmed semiotic practice of our culture. The desire for immediate coherence that necessarily accompanies the use of the thematic code prohibits the access to differences that our object of study demands. Hence the necessity to proceed to yet another leap by abduction, this time in supposing the validity of the gender code. The position of the gender code is different from that of the thematic code. The latter is not institutionalized in any discipline, but disciplines adopt it freely. The gender code is adopted, most often in its masculine version, without ever being avowed. Only since the development of women's studies is it both criticized and explicitly embraced: in its feminist version, of course. A gender code is the code of a group, masculine or feminine, the members of which belong simultaneously to other groups whose codes they also use. When implicit, the gender code will have the same characteristics as the moral code. Anachronistic, it will project a group's reactions upon a text that does not belong to this group. As legitimate as such a procedure may be under certain precise conditions, it does not meet the criteria adopted for the purposes of the present comparative examination. When explicit, on the other hand, the gender code will be justified by the effort it makes to join the gender code of the text; the latter will then have to be distinguished from the code of the group. Only then can the characteristics shared by the group directing the interpretation and the group assumed to be represented by the subject of the text be distinguished from the characteristics that differentiate them. Such an analysis of groups and of the interests that determine their cultural expression requires the cooperation of different disciplines. What follows from this necessity is the natural interdisciplinarity of the semiotic interpretation of ancient texts. The complex relationships between the semiotic subject who is the author of a text, and the codes linked to the different groups of which this subject is a member, are ambiguous. I will not hesitate, in order to emphasize the concept of the code to which I am subscribing in this study, to personify it. This personification is a mode of expression that prompts us to reflect constantly on the dimensions of the individual freedom of the semiotic subject, governed by the authority of codes that s/he in turn helps to perpetuate.

·I·

DISCIPLINARY CODES

The disciplinary specialization we know today is only a few decades old and, in the most general sense, dates back perhaps some two and a half centuries. Already it is extremely difficult for us to imagine that specialization was not always the norm, and today interdisciplinarity has the ring of something new, even revolutionary. If there is innovation here, however, it lies in the disciplinary consciousness attendant upon every interdisciplinary endeavor, that consciousness which permits us to distinguish our own interpretive acts. It is to emphasize the productivity of that consciousness that I intend to analyze, in the pages that follow, a number of common disciplinary operations. The disciplinary codes selected are those whose relevance to my project is beyond doubt. There are other codes whose importance can indeed be justified but that are the subject of greater dissent, like the psychoanalytic code, which I think is highly relevant to the present case but which would give rise to the kind of debate that could only hinder the progress of our present discussion (see Bal 1984b). I have eliminated still other codes because they are relevant only in part, like the medical code and the archaeological code; capable, each in its own way, of contributing to the interpretation of details in the texts, they do not provide us with the larger picture, a comprehensive perspective.

The Hebrew Bible has been regarded simultaneously as many things: historiographic document, theological testimony, reflection of the modes of life of an ancient people, and "popular" literary text. The disciplinary codes whose importance stands out immediately in this characterization are the historical, theological, anthropological, and literary codes. These, therefore, will provide the material for the analysis that follows.

·1·

THE HISTORICAL CODE

Two kinds of historical research can immediately be distinguished: the historical criticism of texts, and the historiography of the Israelite people. The intimate connection between the two constitutes both the importance and the problematic character of the use of the historical code for the interpretation of biblical texts; nevertheless, the relationship between text and history differs in the two cases.

Historical criticism seeks to establish the history of the formation of the corpus by means of the method known as "separation of sources." Proceeding from the hypothesis of a long, diffuse, and complex genesis, this approach divides the text into sections. Different fragments are attributed to different sources: an oral folkloric base, an act of compilation, a composition serving a theological or historiographic intention, a belated insertion into a given book. How can this procedure be considered a code? The hypothesis of the fractured text does not itself act directly as an interpretative rule, but is rather at the source of more detailed hypotheses, which in turn govern the method. Strongly personified hypothetical subjects are constructed on the basis of these hypotheses. In the historical-critical discourse on Judges, the figure of the "deuteronomistic redactor," also called the "deuteronomistic historian," is so systematically emphasized that it is fair to characterize him as a hero. This character, invested with specific capacities, confronted by problems that figure as adversaries, is presumed to have an *intention* whose fulfillment constitutes, in the discourse of the historical-critical school, "his" narrative program. It is this hypothetical teleology that constitutes the disciplinary code. In its major points the discussion on Homer is analogous.

In contrast to the historical-critical school, historiography uses texts as eyewitness documents whose historicity is being tested. The history of the establishment of the Israelites as the dominant people of "the promised land" constitutes the background against which the episodes of the book of Judges unfold. The historian is concerned with untangling the facts from the myths, the true from the false, and therefore his/her interpretation of the text will be openly suspicious. Among the many theories on the "conquest" of Canaan (Miller 1977:264), some will bring the historian closer to the text than others. The most recent, for exam-

15

ple, which postulates an internal rebellion of peasants, will lead the interpreter to regard the text, woven upon the loom of war, as something entirely mythical, and the "war of Yahweh" represented in Judges as a fiction with ideological tendencies. The interpretation based on this theory will be very different from that which proceeds from the theory of the Exodus and the pan-Israelite invasion. For the latter, the difference between the tribes enumerated in the song and those named elsewhere in the text will be extremely significant. The hypothesis of Alt's school (1967), which posits a progressive and generally peaceful penetration of nomads in search of grazing land (Weippert 1971, 1972), will influence the interpretation of the scene of the murder, situated in Jael's tent. If we accept the thesis of migrations of autonomous tribal groups (school of Albright, 1968), we will consider chapter 4 to be more reliable than the song, which, from this point of view, would exaggerate the unity of the tribes. Historical research thus uses the theories that it builds like so many codes, just as historical-critical research employs the intentional subject it constructs as a code.

A third group of interpretive acts will be briefly introduced in this chapter. Here I mean the use of history itself, of the presupposition of historicity, as a rule of correlation between signs and content. In certain cases, this presupposition serves to justify the moral instincts of the historian, who is then free to pass judgment on the murder. We will see that in such evaluative pronouncements, the conflict between two interests, one tied to a specific gender, the other religious or nationalist, will force scientific discourse to give way to a discourse that is highly emotive. In other cases, the premise of historicity paradoxically leads to anachronism. This is what happens in discourses that are simultaneously explanatory and evaluative, discourses that juxtapose, in order to compare them, historical figures from greatly distant periods. In this group one chiefly finds popularizing texts that invoke disciplinary historical research for their own ends.

The History of the Texts

Richter's study (1963), the second half of which is partly reconsidered in Richter (1964), is exemplary in several respects. It represents one of the classic works of the historical-critical school on the book of Judges, analyzing chapters 3–9 in greatest detail. It has often been cited and reevaluated, and certain of its presuppositions are regarded as definitive (Mayes 1983). In addition, Richter later elaborated his method in a systematic manual (1971) that enables us to follow its steps. Richter's works are taken here as a paradigmatic example of the disciplinary code in question. This choice does not imply any judgment of their value. The selection, I must admit, has its paradoxical side to the extent that Richter's enterprise is not hermeneutic. His description of the fragments is highly formal, and the absence of interpretations in the presentation of his results is remarkable. All the same, the interpretative act is there. Without being openly admitted, it is the unexpressed point of departure; this inversion, as I hope to prove, only serves to augment the restrictive power of the code.

The historical-critical school's *modus operandi* includes the following procedures (Miller 1976:14, lists them in reverse order):

1. *Textual criticism,* that is, the analysis of the stages of the written tradition; this critical procedure attempts to trace the successive transformations of the text after its initial composition.
2. *"Literary" criticism,* which is concerned with larger and most often composite entities, whose sources, dates of composition, authors, and intentions it attempts to reconstruct.
3. *History of the tradition,* which devotes itself to the stages, most often oral, of the transmission of the texts; for instance, the migration of motifs and genres.
4. *Criticism of form,* which explores the social context and the functions that genres and various literary forms exercise within it.

It goes without saying that, given the present state of the sources, the practitioners of the school are forced to resort to sometimes spectacular hypotheses. However, we are not concerned here with the methodological problems inherent in the discipline. Rather, the task before us is to analyze the intervention of the hermeneutic process in the course of these disciplinary procedures, and the consequences of this intervention for the interpretative act that addresses the difference between the two fragments describing the murder. It is clear that this school begins with the premise of differentiation itself, since its objective is the *separation* of sources. The polemic stance it assumes vis-à-vis the presupposition of the unity of inspiration or, worse, of the divine voice, predominant in romantic biblical research before the rise of the school, seems promising. Let us consider its position regarding the triad of unity, difference, and interpretation.

According to Willis (1979:845), it is important not to underestimate the activities of the redactors, who, contrary to what an editor does today, visibly intervened in the texts. We recognize the same procedure in medieval European manuscripts. Their task was not confined to the presentation of material. They commented upon it, interpreted it, arranged it in order to give it a certain coherence, and removed or added elements when they felt it was necessary. They added, for example, the introductions and the recapitulations at the end of fragments, in order to reinforce the unity of the corpus. These supplements are referred to as *frameworks;* their function consists not only in establishing connections between the fragments but moreover in relating them to the redactor's own historiographical and theological concerns. According to the specialists of this school, the redactors must have gone even further, elaborating, in a truly authorial capacity, the integrated construction of the compositions. The school goes as far as holding them responsible for the parallels, repetitions, echoes, and retrospective passages that integrate the text.

This labor, whose traces seem to be quite clear in the book of Judges, constitutes only the final step in a long process, regarded by the historian as diachronic, spread out over several centuries. What matters to the historian is to reconstruct that process, even with almost nothing to speak of but traces of the very last stage. The historian of this school begins with a hypothetical scheme that codifies the structure of the process; reconstruction means moving backwards through the sequence. This hypothesis can be summarized as follows (Willis 1979:85):

—The first stage to reconstruct is the cultural background in which the tradition was introduced. The importance of this background is crucial: it determines the expectations of the audience, who in turn incite the "jongleurs" to adapt to the form, the genre, and the content that are comprehensible and expected.
—Having established the background, one assumes that there must have been a crucial event within that background—an event of political, meteorological, social, or cultural significance—which gave birth to the tradition. This event could also have been the first enunciation of a song, a prayer, a maxim.
—Then, the crucial event must have been conserved in the collective memory of the group.
—Several of these recollections were combined before the writing of the book where they now have their place.
—Only as a final step, the work of the redactor described above ensued, in a by now very different cultural milieu and social class.

The penultimate stage is visible, according to Richter (1963, 1964), in the book of Judges, which he divides, on the basis of this hypothesis, into several sections: a true and very brief book of judges; a number of supplements without connection to the rest (chapters 17–21); and his own particular object of study, an ancient collection "of deliverers," as it is called, a *Retterbuch* that is to be distinguished from the book of Judges. Our two chapters represent part of this last ancient stratum. In chapter 3 I will return to the concept of the judge, for the most part generally accepted, which underlies this distinction. What is important here is to see the presuppositions of the hypothesis as a whole and to understand their consequences for the interpretation of the two versions.

It is clear that the evolution outlined depends a great deal upon "common sense," whose illusions, however, it also implies. It is in the interaction presupposed in the first three stages that preconceptions concerning the notion of history insert themselves. Within these three stages it is not difficult to see that a dialectical process between the general and the particular, the collective and the individual, the traditional and the original is predicated; a model of thought that, in its binary structure, is part of the modern Occidental tradition. Without wanting to deny the importance of a cultural background as a "horizon of expectation," we may question the legitimacy of the image of the poet "obliged" to "adapt" to this background. What of the poet in the service of the emerging state, whose task was to subtly modify this horizon of expectation? Next, the singularity of the "crucial event" of the second stage precludes the possibility of a collective creation; it isolates the unique Event as the figure that inaugurates tradition. It seems clear to me that this aspect of the hypothesis functions to defend the potential historicity if not of the event itself, political or other, at least of the occasion of its enunciation. The underlying individualism of the hypothesis leaves little place for the collective imagination: collectivity is accorded the secondary role of receptacle of creation and guardian of tradition. The contribution of the historian, who tries to verify the factual historicity of the event, is biased from the very start by this structure of thought. We shall see how this factor affects the interpretive act.

The hypothesis is embraced by Richter in his studies of the *Retterbuch;* his method is later made explicit (1971). The criteria for the separation of sources, Richter insists, must be evaluated before the analysis of form and genre. It is striking that philology, in the strict sense of the term, enjoys only a minor role in his procedure. The knowledge of the evolution of the Hebrew language is, according to him, too sparse, and too often philological hypotheses are based upon a study of the distribution of words in fragments originally separated to avoid circularity. He cites the common distinction between the uses of the divine names Yahweh and Elohim (1971:55), which is generally accepted but has led astray many historians of the text. Among the criteria Richter applies for the separation of sources, the foremost are lexical repetitions, phrases (formulae), and motifs; tensions and contradictions; the difference between fragments with parallel composition and fragments with disparate composition; the preponderance of an abstract as opposed to a concrete vocabulary; and parallels that sometimes take the form of doublings. By means of these criteria, Richter divides the text into fragments of diverse origins.

Applied to the two versions of the murder, the criteria lead the critic to
conclude that chapter 4 is composite, while the song, from verse 6 to
verse 30, is a unity, framed only by the redactor in the last sentence. Let
us see how these criteria are used. Turning to the narrative, Richter
observes that there is only one principal character. The focus is suc-
cessively displaced from Jabin to Deborah, to Barak, to Sisera, to Jael.
We will later see that this progressive displacement of interest serves as
the starting point for a literary study of the structure of the narrative.
Guided by his historical code, however, Richter sees in this distribution
of narrative interest a sign for which the content /diverse sources/ imposes itself. Richter comments (1963:44):

> Diese Tendenzveränderung, die sich nicht darauf beschränkt, in
> einzelnen Szenen verschiedene Personen abwechselnd in der Vord-
> dergrund zu stellen, ohne deshalb die Wertung zu verändern, worin
> sich den Kompositionswille eines Verfassers zeigte, sondern auch die
> ganz neue Schwerpunkte setzt, kann kaum einem Verfasser zuge-
> schrieben werden.

> This change of tendency, which is not limited to alternately highlight-
> ing different characters within specific scenes, without, however,
> changing their evaluation—in a procedure of this kind, the composi-
> tional intention of the author would reveal itself—but which, in addi-
> tion, establishes entirely new culminating points, could hardly be at-
> tributed to a single author.

The critic, wishing to limit his analysis to a purely scientific description,
abstains from an evaluation of the act of Jael. He restricts himself to
classifying the passage 4:18–22 as an autonomous genre, whose function
he describes as follows (1963:49): "Das Ziel der kleinen Episode ist wohl
die Heldentat Jaels, jedoch ist sie nur ein Glied aus den Taten des Barak"
(It is true that the objective of the little episode is the heroic act of Jael,
but this is only one element [member] of the acts of Barak). Even if the
last citation seems colored by the desire—linked to a specific gender—to
reduce the importance of the feminine character, it is not this particular
aspect that interests me here. What captures the attention in this meeting
of criteria and text is the vital contribution of prior interpretation,
founded in turn upon certain preconceptions. Richter's evaluation is
surely based, implicitly and undoubtedly unbeknownst to the critic himself, on the projection upon this very ancient text of a conception of the
epic not quite so ancient. Even Zumthor (1983), who defuses many a
modern prejudice in his excellent study, defines the epic genre thus
(105): "L'épopée met en scène l'aggressivité virile au service de quelque
grande enterprise" (The epic depicts virile aggressiveness in the service
of some great enterprise). Zumthor is not unaware of the limited historical value of such a definition. It is difficult, however, to exclude the
historical books of the Bible from the genre for which the Homeric epic

still constitutes the paradigm. What to do, then, with a text where this "virile" aggressiveness belongs to a woman, and where the man is less heroic than the genre could wish? Separate the sources.

The shifting focus, highlighting now this character, now that, falls within the domain of the criterion of "tensions and contradictions." Since the chapter is consecrated to collective battle—the "great enterprise"—the scene of the murder committed in private is merely a secondary part of that enterprise; since Barak is commander of the army, he must be the principal character of the entire chapter. Obviously the initial interpretive act consists in declaring war to be the thematic subject of the narrative. Once this decision is made, only the hero of the narrative can be the commander of the army. The same conclusion is often drawn by others; Keil and Delitzsch (1980:238) go so far as to say: "the glorious victory . . . through the judge Deborah and the heroic warrior Barak . . . so fully described in Deborah's triumphal song," without seeming to realize that Barak hardly appears in the song at all. Richter's study offers the advantage of explaining this interpretation. The choice of theme is linked to the hypothesis of the crucial event. This event is the climax of the "great enterprise," which itself must be entrusted to virile aggressiveness—according to our definition of the epic. The presupposed dialectic between the unique and the general implies that only an event of this magnitude is capable of retaining the attention of the collectivity charged with conserving it. In this way the historian of the text joins the historian of the people.

We can oppose this argument while remaining faithful to the same system—the criterion of "tensions." Why should not the scene of the murder represent the culminating point of an event that circumscribes ever more closely the motif of war, eliminating characters who are officially established but inadequate, and progressively centering on the doubly marginal heroine—a woman and a foreigner—who draws her power from this position? This interpretation can only be excluded by taking two basic oppositions for granted, both integral parts of the hypothesis of the crucial event: that between public and private, and that between the historical, conceived as the political history of the people, and the imaginary, conceived as irrelevant. Nevertheless, there is no reason whatsoever to distinguish these domains *a priori,* especially when their separation, and its importance for the political situation, is represented as crucial. We have only to imagine that the "cultural background" of the first stage maintained an integrated interest in the movements between all these domains, which were not separable for the public—the collective creator—in order to perceive, on the contrary, the refinement of the composition.

The example exposes, in the underlying interpretive act, other conceptions inherent in the program of the historical-critical school, again following from its initial hypothesis. The criteria elaborated lend themselves to organization into two categories. The first—repetitions and parallels—decides that there is a divergence of sources from the moment an element is not new. The second—tensions, contradictions, and differences of vocabulary—decides that there is divergence from the moment an element is new. Difference is positive relative to unity for the first category, negative for the second. Rather than seeing this either as paradox or contradiction, what matters here is to understand how the two categories are related.

The examples most often cited regarding repetition as a criterion for the separation of sources of a given text is that of the double narrative of the creation, in Genesis 1 and 2 respectively. I have tried to show elsewhere (1987) that even if one concludes, on philological grounds, for example, that there are two divergent origins, the two narratives are neither contradictory nor repetitive; on the contrary. The hypothesis of repetition always depends in part upon a linear conception of diachrony, a conception not *a priori* compatible with the poetics of the book of Genesis. Alter (1981), who defends the unity of Genesis 1 and 2 on other grounds than I, offers a large number of examples of "repetitions" alleged by the historical-critical school, and effectively refutes them. The criterion itself, just as much as the underlying idea, is based on a conception of literariness that is not *a priori* applicable to an ancient text. This conception demands *originality*. At its height during the romantic period, it owes much, according to Lotman (1973), to the aesthetic of difference, which alternates dialectically with the aesthetic of identity in the Occidental tradition—both premises themselves resting upon a defective reading of Aristotle's concept of mimesis (Bal 1982). I will return to this idea in chapter 3. But the tenacity of this aesthetic must have even deeper roots.

Tensions and contradictions, which at first glance seem to point toward an opposing system of values, not only stem from the same aesthetic conception, but, what is more, they form an integral part of the same criterion, and their application is as powerfully tied to the bias of the critic. The verdict that finds Genesis 1 and 2 guilty of *repetition* is based upon a *contradiction*—illusory, in my view—between the two versions of the creation of woman. As soon as the contradiction is neutralized, the repetition disappears. The tension signaled by Richter in Judges 4 between 10–18, the public event, and 18–22, the private event, originates, we have seen, from the premise of the great event, which underlies the central hypothesis of the school, and disappears as soon as this anachronistic rule of the critic is suspended. Nevertheless, even if he persists in seeing tension, only a desire to do away with difference can bring the critic to consider it a criterion for the separation of sources.

The apparent paradox in the position described dissolves, not only at the practical level we have just analyzed but also at the theoretical level, as soon as one perceives how the two categories are in fact two sides of the same conception of literature. Todorov (1981) and Genette (1976), like many others, have effectively demonstrated it: both unity and originality constitute part of an *organic* conception of literature. Thus, the positivist critical historian does not escape from the ancestral romantic roots to which he is opposed.

Richter accepts the composite character of the narrative in contrast to the unified song. The last conclusion may strike us as surprising; the song contains at least as many repetitions. But the critic arrives at his conclusion through the analysis of genres, which, although mixed in both cases, are, he believes, autonomous in 4, while interdependent in 5. Blenkinsopp (1961), following the same argument, comes to precisely the opposite conclusion: the song, he believes, represents a combination of original epic elements and of hymnic elements indicative of a belated liturgical elaboration. The anachronism committed here is criticized by Lind (1980:66), who seeks to rejoin the "cultural base" by a comparison with neighboring cultures. "The unity of hymnic and epic features in Near Eastern victory-odes is the rule, not the exception." And, indeed, this mixture is characteristic of the ode, which commemorates (epic) an event with enthusiasm (lyric). Despite the problems of the comparative approach, the desire to transcend the narrowly evolutionist hypothesis opens up the discipline, truly a most welcome effect. Even if a diffuse evolution of the canon is highly probable, an analysis governed by an anachronistic conception of unified literary genres depends only superficially upon the notion of historical progression.

In order to see the *code* characteristic of this discipline at work, one last aspect of the example of Richter is worth considering. In the ensemble of the German's works, personifications are frequent. This figure is an index of importance; never innocent, it gives a specific sense to the discourse that employs it. I already stated this point concerning my own personifications of the concept of the code: they suggest a specific conception of the relative (lack of) freedom of the subject in language. Let us see how they function in Richter's work, and what relations they establish between the different elements of his overall conception. The subject here is the *intention* attributed to fragment 4:18–22, distinguished, in the historical-critical discourse, from the intention of the whole chapter. As the distinction leads the critic to embrace the conclusion of the fragmented origin of the text, that text as a whole can be attributed only to a relatively recent redactor. Therefore, it is he who, according to this view, would have felt the need to subordinate the act of Jael to the great political event. In this way the personification both personifies *and* historicizes the unexpressed and undoubtedly unconscious ideology of the critic. This personification of the editorial process is indeed striking.

Mayes (1983) incorporates Richter's lesson and takes it further. In a systematic study of the history of Israel according to the deuteronomistic historians, he subscribes to Richter's theory. He sketches an entire ideology, sometimes even a psychology, of the figure of the deuteronomist, who is said to have had as his goal "to provide a stimulus and support for the traditional holy war ideal" (164). The redactor thus envisioned would have made use of traditional material toward this end. Here is still another argument that supports the subordination of the murder, originating from older and irretrievable sources, to that which alone is relevant for the historian, the narrative of warfare.

The personification of the intention of hypothetical author has been common practice in literary studies since Booth (1961) introduced the term *implied author*. This term salvaged from the ruins of nineteenth-century literary history, demoralized and supplanted by the new reigning theory of immanence, the very factor that was at the source of its collapse: intention. Free of the biographical responsibilities necessarily attached to the notion of the author, the idea of the implied author was welcomed with a suspect enthusiasm. It permitted the integration of this rebaptized author within the autonomist current. Thus the circularity for which literary history was reproached in times past still perpetuates itself today. The problem has been pointed out several times (Pelc 1971; Bal 1981b); it consists in misusing the model of communication by inverting it. The part of reception, which is to say, the interpretation of the reader-analyst (hence, the result of the code), is projected upon the part of emission, where the sender chooses the codes in order to construct a message. The confusion is obvious. A circularity ensues, which the personification of the intention of the "implied author" serves to mask, and where the interpreter inevitably sees his own interpretation confirmed. Thus, the conventional image of the origin of texts, an image colored by romantic ideas of the poetic genius before an enthusiastic public, is revised. First, the original creation will be corrected by a theologian of greater wisdom or by a historian of greater expertise than this archaic poet. Then, the creative act takes the form of a man, our friend the deuteronomist, who, as if by a miracle, executes exactly the procedures imagined by the interpreter, just to confirm the modern interpretation. This beautiful tale is, alas, a little too beautiful.

This outline of its method does not propose to abandon altogether the work of the historical-critical school. Rather it seeks to expose its illusions. It seems to me of great importance to clearly distinguish the role of the interpretive acts and that of the codes directing them, in order to discover their precise heuristic value. Here a word on methodology in its semiotic aspect is in order. In the example just analyzed, we can distinguish first a historical code—the hypothesis of five stages—and then different intervening codes. We have seen, for example, that the code that prescribes the separation of the scene of the murder from the narrative of warfare is a modern literary code. The code that, next, authorizes the hierarchization of the two parts is a particular historical code that has been challenged for at least a decade now: that which limits history to politics in the narrow sense. Last of all, a gender code inextricably bound to the preceding ones completes the elaboration of the structure: the act of the woman serves only to glorify all the more that of the man, heroic by definition—even if, at times, by procuration. The personification of the presumed teleology provides the collaboration of the three codes with a disciplinary justification that no longer puts in doubt the legitimacy of its own presuppositions. Thus, the search for *origin*, the hypothesis of a *diachronic* process, and the consequent *subordination* of one fragment to another all assume the incontestability of axioms. The disciplinary code can do nothing now but close off interpretation.

Two misunderstandings are likely to surface at this point. First, one might believe that I claim to have proven the unity of the two chapters. Nothing could be further from the truth. The distinctions set forth by Richter can be established on grounds other than his. I have only sought to show how these arguments are anchored in the modern preconceptions of the researcher, not in the text, so that any conclusion can be deformed by this incongruity. To put it another way, the result of my negative analysis proves nothing positive. This is all the better, for, to move on to the second possible misunderstanding, I am concerned neither with seeking unity nor with finding it. It would be a strange kind of progress indeed to return to the errors of the past and maintain the unity of the biblical texts. What I have attempted to demonstrate is quite the contrary, that behind the fractured text of historical criticism a new unity emerges, personified in the figure of the redactor, but equally established by the critic's own desire for knowledge. For if one *knows* the fractures, one has already repaired them.

Recognized as fundamentally *literary* and *modern*, the basic code of the discipline would make it possible to follow the life of biblical texts in modern society. Moreover, the results, recognized as interpretive and rid of their positivist illusions, could provide the elements of a differentiating critical interpretation. Even in a confused or unsound analysis, the highlighting of the scene of the murder, different in the two versions, has a certain heuristic value. It puts us on the track of an aspect that will prove interesting: the texts' different attitudes in the face of the murder, an event surrounded in the narrative by circumstantial complements, embraced in the song without reservations. Understood in this way, the historical-critical code and Richter's study, which is one of its creations, assume an entirely new meaning, one in which criticism inspires self-criticism. A differential reading of the text can only be possible on such a basis.

The History of the People

The historiographic disclosure adopts two attitudes toward the text of Judges. Either it starts from the documentary value of isolated texts, and discusses the differences between 4 and 5 as a problem of relative truth, or it considers the composition of the entire book as a testimonial act. The history to be reconstructed in the first case is that of the establishment of the people in the land, and in the second, that of the kingdom, justifying itself by the narrative of its own past. The two attitudes display varying degrees of confidence in the texts as sources. In addition, among the historians studying the establishment in Palestine, greatly diverse theories compete, which, in turn, serve as codes leading to extremely varied interpretations. It is out of the question here to study all the current positions. Codes being our present object of study, only those interpretive acts which reflect particular hypotheses will be considered.

The first concern of the historian is the relative and absolute dating of fragments and events; it is here that the two historical disciplines meet. In general, the song is acknowledged to be the older of the two versions. From there to the attribution of greater documentary value is a large step, one that the cautious historian is not always ready to take; others are not so reluctant to take it, if only implicitly. Mayes (1974:88), who follows Richter closely in his division and his arguments, arrives at the conclusion of an inverted hierarchy: regarding the sections of the narrative (whose partition was shown to be problematic), "There seems no doubt . . . that these sections must be taken as quite distinct, and that the priority should be assigned to the final section 18–22, insofar as it *stands closest to the event*" (my italics). The italicized expression is ambiguous. Mayes supports it with a literary argument: the representation is more detailed, the language more vivid and colorful, and the event particularized; we can thus rely on it for a greater historical precision. As the fragment is also supposed to be the oldest, the expression "closest to the event" suggests a chronological proximity that guarantees, in turn, a relative contemporaneity and the fidelity of the description. The detailed language thus assures the connection between two distinct domains. Is the event depicted in detail and/or/because with precision? What is in question, in this ambiguity, is the connection between one isotopy—the "real" event, painted with precision (exactitude)—and another—the (fictive?) event, represented with precision (in detail). In the first case, one can retrieve the history, in the second, the imagination of the people. Let us leave this ambiguity, for the moment, unresolved.

The attempt to fix dates is quickly abandoned by the same historian when he compares the two versions, which are, according to him, inconsistent (1977:312): "The serious differences between the two accounts, especially in relation to the participants in the battle, are not open to any harmonization." The discrepancy in question concerns the list, in the song, of the participating tribes, which is flagrantly opposed to the two tribes named in the narrative. As the song is older, the greater number of tribes it mentions has been received with enthusiasm by the adherents of the theory of the pan-Israelite invasion as support for their cause. It has given rise to Noth's theory (1930), already old, of an Israelite amphic-tyony based on the Greek model. Such an association of twelve tribes organized around a central sanctuary is today considered improbable, and Noth's arguments, often drawn from Judges 5, are not, indeed, very convincing (De Geus 1976; Mayes 1974, 1983). The hypothesis and the discussion it has provoked are interesting as an example of interpreta-tion. The song of Deborah mentions only ten tribes; the problem was how to accommodate this "anomaly." Chronology came to the rescue: it was not until after the battle against Sisera—and before the monarchy—that the amphictyony came into being.

Mayes (1974) refutes Noth's arguments one by one without, however, questioning the relationship between text and history that they presup-posed. First, the theory is based upon the number of tribes, twelve, whose significance for the mythology of Israel is well known. The Greek amphictyony, however, could comprise a lesser or greater number of tribes. The historian, adopting the number twelve as a code, makes the task unnecessarily difficult, forced as he/she is to question the historical value of the list of the song, and hence of the entire song. The number twelve is evidently based on other biblical passages, in which the list of tribes is either absent or of a later date. The desire to make the theory compatible with the myth becomes manifest. Next, the concept of *judge* is used as an argument by Noth, a counterargument by Mayes, but neither one exploits the possibility offered by the narrative, where the function is again described with more precision, of questioning the generally ac-cepted separation of "judge" and "liberator" (see, however, chapter 3 of the present study). The debate's point of contention remains the ques-tion of the origin of national unity, a significant feature of the song as opposed to the narrative. It is perhaps even the reason for the integra-tion of the song into the canon. Historians dispute the nature of this unity, its origin, and its status at the epoch described. In its capacity to blind the interpreter to other questions, to confer a unique and institu-tional sense upon the text, this point of contention is invested with the function and the power of a code.

We can imagine the skepticism regarding the text to be even more radical in the historian subscribing to the theory of peaceful establish-ment. This is the case for Weippert (1979:32), who attributes the repre-sentation in the books of Joshua and Judges to a more recent interpreta-tion. This position seems to attest to an "objective" scientific attitude: the historian refuses to be influenced by mythology. As an interpretive act,

the decision to sever all connections between history and the texts is
directed by a code whose implications for critical reading are of great
significance. It invalidates the importance and the historic reality of the
imagination. The antagonists, adhering to incompatible theories, can at
least agree on this. This is the common code they share; we already saw it
operating in the work of Richter, prescribing a hierarchy between the
political history descriptive of events and the cultural history of the people, a hierarchy based upon a conception of politics contradicted elsewhere. It is applied very selectively: it is certainly not about heroic acts
like Ehud's that remarks like Soggin's (1981:68) are made: "and this
climax, with its *individualistic, anecdotal, apolitical* character, also suggests
the perspective in which the two texts 4 and 5 should be read: they are
not history, but epic" (my italics). The remark is not one that leads the
author to think through the historical status either of the *vision* that is the
epic, or of the "apolitical" and "individualist" character of the narratives
of solitary heroic acts upon which history is nourished. In the same way,
to relegate the list of tribes in the song to the domain of fiction, regarded
with disdain, is to miss the opportunity to learn from fiction, as a document of cultural life, the state of mind of the people out of which the
texts have emerged. The cleavage between two conceptions of history,
one political, the other cultural, remains intact, with all the arbitrariness
it implies. Thus there is no difference in *code* between the skeptics and
the historians who are followers of other theories. In every case, the text
that most faithfully reflects the central thesis of the theory will be declared the most reliable: the song for the theory of the amphictyony; the
narrative for the theory of intertribal wars and the protracted penetration of isolated tribes; and neither one for both the theory of peaceful
settlement and that of the peasant revolt.

There is another historical approach, proposed by Weiser (1959), that
holds interest for the discussion of codes. In order to reduce the difference between the two versions, he proposes for the song a pragmatic
analysis of the situation of enunciation as code. The code gives rise to the
interpretation of the song as a cultic celebration of the event. Those
tribes reproached for their absence would have failed to participate not
in the battle, which is presumed to have concerned only the two tribes
mentioned in the narrative, Zebulon and Naphtali, but in the cult. These
two tribes indeed figure twice in the song, at verse 14, where their presence at the festival would have been praised, and at verse 18, which
would refer to the actual battle. This distinction, according to Weiser,
would explain not only the difference between the two versions, but also
that between the light reproach and the sterner condemnation of Meroz
(5:23), who, allied to both participating tribes, should have fought with
them.

Paradoxically, this interpretation, which openly seeks to harmonize the two versions, differentiates them much more than the preceding approaches. It is true that Weiser does not dwell on the problems of a comparison between two texts of different genres and epochs (Mayes 1974:87) and that he therefore proceeds to some extent upon questionable methodological foundations. Nevertheless, and it is in this respect that his work holds interest for us, he performs two important interpretive acts. First, in suggesting the possibility of a cultural event in his discussion of tribes, Weiser makes use of a more open conception of historical reality. He is thus able to distinguish two distinct acts of reference in the discourse of the poetess, and to establish a diachrony of events that replaces the hierarchy whose illegitimacy we have seen. This conception of history as code has, therefore, more differentiating power. This is precisely what Weiser's critics fail to see when they resituate the debate within the opposition between the political history and the cultural history of which the cult is a part. In addition, the discussion that opposes cultic interpretation to historical interpretation presupposes that the Yahwist's redaction was equally important for both texts. It thus ignores the theology peculiar to the song; this is a subject to which we will return. Second, the pragmatic code that interprets the text as a product of the situation of enunciation offers several advantages. Without getting stuck in endless speculations on the history of the text, Weiser acknowledges the situation of enunciation as an integral part of the history enunciated. He integrates the context, the speaker, and the receiver in the meaning of the text. This integration will turn out to be extremely fruitful for the interpretation of differences between the two versions. I will return to it in chapter 3. Thus, even while seeking to reconcile the two versions, and even while neglecting generic differences in the act of comparison, the historian has projected in his analysis a historical-pragmatic code that is highly differential.

The opposition whose tenacity has been observed is all the more remarkable in that it relentlessly poses problems for the historians of the Israelite people. Gottwald (1979:73), who supports the theory of the peasant revolt, formulates the problem in this way:

> Up to the present, biblical studies have grappled with a model of the settlement and with a model of the cultic production of traditions, but there has been no adequate mediation between these two forms of inquiry within a larger analytic model of the social system involved in the twin process of taking power in the land and of building its own traditions.

Even while remaining insufficiently analytic, Weiser's approach situates itself in the program enunciated here. What is missing, if the mediation that Gottwald demands is to be established, is a *historical* interpretation of ideological evolution. If we look at the Bible as a document not of political history in the narrow sense but of ideological history, then we see at once to what degree the tensions observed by the critics are thematized in the texts.

In an entirely different context, Patrick (1979:146–47) discusses the coexistence of two models of explanation of the origin of the people: the model of the patriarchs and the model of the Exodus. The first is built on the tension between *election* and *heredity*. This tension manifests itself not just in the numerous cases where the second son takes the place of the first. It is also at hand when a foreigner, a woman, or a foreign woman fulfills the crucial function of saving the continuity of history. The different forms that this tension assumes are combined in the story of Tamar, Genesis 38, and in that of Ruth (see Bal 1987 for an extended analysis of these two cases). The status of Jael warrants examination from this perspective.

Besides this *familial* model, the model of the *Exodus,* founded on the motif of the liberation from oppression, represents the *political* tension between *conquest* and the imperialism it implies, and *sympathy for the oppressed.* Speculating what could have "really" happened in the double narrative of the battle against Sisera is not in this sense the proper task of the historian; but the place that each version occupies in the ideological history, where the two models constantly interact in a thousand different ways, constitutes a legitimate question of historical research. This would be the macrostructure of the entire Bible as Patrick envisions it; conversely, the way he envisions it would serve as code for such an interpretation. The position of Deborah in relation to Barak, of Jael in relation to Barak, of the two women within the enterprise of the establishment in the land, whether factual or imaginary, should be examined from this perspective.

We have seen that the historiographic code is allied to rather questionable ideological positions. These stances privilege political history as the succession of concrete military events. They separate the cultural life of the people from the public life of its leaders, passing over the first in silence. They ignore the importance of the private domain as well as of the collective imagination. These positions have generated the epic genre in the narrow sense just as much as they have influenced the modern conception of that genre. The agreement between the two leads modern scholars to valorize this genre so close to their own preoccupations, going so far as to declare it the primitive form and source of all literature. The imagination, which is nevertheless the principal source of the single text-document we possess, is isolated, ignored, or devaluated. It is that imagination, however, which will prove capable of illuminating the fundamental difference between the two versions, a difference that, in turn, is crucial to our comprehension of the historical past.

Connoted History

In concluding, it seems important to briefly examine the way the historical discourse is adopted to mask other less acknowledgeable orientations, especially in the popularizing commentaries. First, it is striking to see how the historical code enters into competition with other codes. As soon as the interpretations result in contradiction, or even when the priority simply seems to deviate from the great political event toward other themes, the historian will more often than not adopt a polemical attitude and set about actively opposing the rival code. For example, recognizing that most specialists agree in acknowledging the song to be a historical source superior to the narrative of chapter 4, Cundall (1968: 92–93) makes the restrictive character of the code explicit, in warning: "It must be remembered that the language of poetry is not always precise; *elaborations* and *hyperboles* are employed to *increase* the effect" (my italics). The description comes straight from the manuals of rhetoric, themselves anchored in a tradition of literacy; moreover, this manner of "discrediting" the lyric code presupposes a particular order of composition and a kind of correlation between the texts that is inherent in a certain prescriptive norm. It is not possible to speak in terms of efforts "to increase the effect," of "elaboration," and of "hyperboles" unless the song is being compared to a certain source; in other words, if it is considered as subsequent to the other source, the narrative. The elements present in 5 and absent in 4 are "elaborations" and "hyperboles" in one case; they are censored or repressed in the other. Moreover, among the three differences, the praise of Jael, the passage on Sisera's mother, and the representation of the victim's death, only the last can truly be described in these terms. Against this devalorization of poetry as source stands the opinion of Freedman (1979:85), who defends it thus: "There are, however, corresponding advantages in poetry roughly contemporary with the events and circumstances: songs often capture the spirit of the occasion and focus on what is centrally important." Poetry gives access to the kind of differential interpretation that Weiser had pointed to, in which the human mental state—the "internal"—once more finds its place. Freedman (86) adds a different argument, which is concerned with reintegrating the two aspects of history:

> Early poems are closer to the events than any surviving prose account; the transmission of poetry tends to be more faithful than that of prose, even though the former may be predominantly an oral phenomenon and the latter a written tradition. This is so because word selection and placement as well as rhythmic and stylistic factors are central in poetic composition and contribute to the preservation of the material in its original form. Contrariwise, except for mechanical blunders, it is easier

to protect the sense of a prose composition, while indulging in editorial revisions.

This argument, which will reappear in chapter 3, is important here for the conservative character it ascribes to poetic form, which better guarantees preservation; it refutes Cundall's suspicion. It suggests, moreover, a different relationship between each version and the work of the redactor. We will see that this difference is crucial for the theological interpretation of the two texts. Even so, Freedman oversimplifies a little when he writes that the sense of prose composition is "easier to protect." It is an *illusion* that this sense is easier to protect, an illusion based on the logocentrism that goes hand in hand with the transition from orality to writing. On the contrary, prose composition helps to convey unperceived the adaptation of the sense to the new ideology.

Cundall turns later to verse 5:6, which evokes the period in question with these words: "In the days of Shamgar the son of Anath, in the days of Jael, the highways were abandoned." Understandably Cundall expresses surprise at "the linking together of the names of Shamgar and Jael," for Shamgar is a minor judge, mentioned only at the end of chapter 3 in a single verse. Another code, for example the psychoanalytic code, would eliminate the surprise, for Shamgar had exterminated six hundred Philistines "with an ox goad," an act whose impact and instrument are similar to Jael's. The mythological code would seek to interpret the complement "son of Anath," which links Shamgar to the Canaanite goddess of war, and would see in Shamgar and Jael a couple symmetrical with Deborah and Barak (Craigie 1972, 1978). But it doesn't matter; much more interesting is Cundall's following remark: "Various emendations have been made to remove the name of Jael from the poem, but none is really satisfactory." One feels that he regrets it. Why, if there is one name too many, try to eliminate that of the more important character? The only explanation imaginable that would leave the good faith of the historian intact would be the priority ascribed to war, which places Shamgar on a par with Barak since they are the two men who killed the greatest number of enemies (even if this means minimizing the role of Deborah in the battle itself). But the effects of restriction and censorship only stand out all the more clearly: historical code and gender code go hand in hand.

Soggin (1981:85) represents an extreme case of the attempt in question. He proposes reading the phrase as "in the time of the yoke," the Hebrew word for "yoke" being close to "Jael." The argument is revealing: "The Hebrew has 'in the time of Jael,' but the woman plays a role only at the end of the song; the mention of her here does not therefore perform any function." First, the devaluation of Jael's role obviously rests upon a narrowly historical interpretation of the text. But the logic becomes truly stupefying when we realize that Shamgar son of Anath plays no role whatsoever in the song. He, however, is not driven out of that song by the philologist with so little respect for the letter of the text.

In the same way, the historical code enters into competition with the narratological code, when Alonso Schökel (1965:162) criticizes the narrative structure of the story. In what is a narratological analysis, the critic implicitly relies upon a conception of war, for his conclusion "So we come to the climax of the action," is justified thus: "For the Israelite believer, the action here attains its summit." The critic then proceeds to condemn the narrative structure for failing to abide by the narrative code, which, in its most restrictive form, would place the climax later. The restriction comes, however, from the historical code, which itself provides the argument on which Alonso Schökel's judgment is based.

The role and very existence of the two women are also obviously at stake in historical interpretations. I will not explore in detail here the function of judge; this question will be studied in an anthropological context. It is in her capacity as military commander that Deborah poses a problem. The appreciation of her role is general: "Deborah, the diviner, was a first-rate military leader, the ideal judge." So writes Boling in his commentary on Judges in the *Anchor Bible* (1975:98). The question is if, as judge, she was exceptional, for apparently there were no other women exercising this function. (There are other prophetesses, Miriam and Hulda; the first was primarily a poetess while the second prophesied, but neither judged.) Boling clarifies that in Mari prophetesses frequently exercised political functions (1975:95); according to him, the introductory verse of the narrative (4:4) evaluates Deborah in the capacity of judge, and "That value judgment was most likely made in the premonarchial period when the simple relationship between the functions of diviner and field commander was a living social reality, but increasingly subject to the mounting pressures for which the arrangement was at last inadequate" (Boling 1975:99). In other words, the growing political and military tensions made the combination of the two functions problematic. Unaddressed here is the question of the sex of the functionary.

Nevertheless, in many commentaries a certain abuse of the historical code is visible in regard to precisely this point. An anachronistic moral evaluation is hidden behind what I call a "connotator of historicity": in this case, the comparison with Joan of Arc. Here is an example, taken from a popularizing source (Gillie and Reid 1924:215):

> The mere fact that Deborah, a woman, was a judge in Israel makes plain that character counted in leadership. It was because of her character she became a leader. *She was not an Amazon.* As she said herself, she was a "Mother in Israel." Her influence was moral and religious, *not physical.* She was indeed brains, and courage, and faith to the warriors. (My italics)

Note the trouble these commentators take to make their readers understand how this state of affairs could have been possible. The negative
formulas (not an Amazon, not physical) betray the source of their own
doubts. They continue in an even more explicit manner:

> And it is remarkable that she became a deliverer without forfeiting her
> womanliness. She was better than Joan of Arc, who could only secure
> victory for her nation by joining the battle. We are taught once more
> that God often chooses unlikely instruments to do His will. (Gillie and
> Reid 1924:215–16)

I could not resist the temptation to include the last sentence, but it is not
the ideology brought into play throughout the passage that interests me
here, nor even the fact that enthusiasm for the femininity of the heroine
leads the authors to abandon their historical code. Nothing proves that
Deborah does not join the battle, if she does not actually lead it. The
comparison with Joan of Arc, frequent in the commentaries, reveals how
the historical code can be exploited. Such a comparison seems to demonstrate fidelity to this code, because Joan is also a celebrated, if not the
most celebrated, heroine of history. However, at the time of La Pucelle, a
female military commander had become a thing of such rarity that she
paid for her initiative with her life. What is more, that in our own era a
team of scholars found it a useful endeavor to initiate a project of interdisciplinary research (lasting ten years) with the goal of proving that
Joan was a man is another example of the abuse of the historical code.
Deborah's position, exceptional as it may be in the Bible, was much more
common in her time than Joan's was in hers. Since historical "truth"
must at least admit the possibility of this position, the comparison with
Joan of Arc contradicts this truth, *under cover* of the historical code. This
comparison accomplishes an inversion of meaning. The message /De-
borah is a great military heroine, better even than Joan of Arc/, whose
denotation would be the historical truth concerning Deborah, is connoted by the comparison, and in fact denotes the exceptional and fictive
character of the phenomenon; more than that, it signifies in connotation
the authentic character of this exceptionality by the appeal to a historical
name. This "effect of the real" (Barthes) serves here to convey an idea
very different from history: that which dictates to women their circumscribed place.

   If the existence and the role of Deborah at least are not challenged, the
same cannot be said for Jael. We have already seen that, according to
Cundall, the attempts to eliminate her name from verse 5:6 of the poem
have been numerous. The preeminence of the set of thematic values
imposed by the historical code as soon as history is considered exclusively
as politics leads the commentators to consider the episode of Jael as

secondary (see Richter and Alonso Schökel), even at the expense of the literary qualities of the text.

Failing the elimination or reduction of Jael's role in the text, still another option remains: to portray her as a criminal, and a notorious one at that. Clearly the moral code comes here to replace the historical code, which is nothing any longer but an accomplice in the role of deceptive connotator of truth—as in the following example: "The heroine of the story is Deborah, a prophetess with the power of a Joan of Arc, who rouses Barak to lead the Northern tribes against Sisera, which he [*sic*] did successfully, and the unfortunate Sisera meets his death at the hands of another [*sic*] bloodthirsty lady" (Gore et al. 1928:156). Once the connotator of truth is introduced, the critic feels free to distort the text. Barak becomes the great conqueror, Sisera is worthy of pity, and Jael is "also" thirsty for blood. Is this to say, as much as Deborah? The negative connotations of *lady* refer precisely to women who do not accept their assigned place. We will have the opportunity to return to the horror that Jael's act seems to inspire in critics who are much less dismayed by similar acts performed by men, such as that of Ehud in chapter 3. Cundall, for example, who calls the act of Jael "one of treachery" (1968:90), praises Ehud in plain language—"Ehud's stratagem was carried out with considerable skill and courage"—praise that could just as well apply to Jael. The connection between the historical code and the moral code peculiar to a specific gender is obvious in the commentary of Keil and Delitzsch (1980). After seven pages of erudite philological and historical notes, one page (306) abruptly intervenes with a moral lesson not quite so erudite. Struggling to explain that Jael's act could not be in accord with the will of Yahweh, they conclude: "her heroic deed cannot be acquitted of the sins of lying, treachery and assassination."

We have seen that the use of the historical code oscillates between two opposing tendencies. The works of the historical-critical school rest on a personified projection of the critic's own literary conception upon the text, and on a biased view of artistic creation. Blindness to his/her own interpretive contribution prevents the historian of the text from seeing all of its possibilities. The underlying literary code is in turn determined by a limited conception of history. The resulting isolation of the scene of the murder can in no way serve a differential interpretation. The scene is by definition subordinated to the great epic representation; this in turn is declared to be of little importance in the chapter, and the historian of the text is left empty-handed.

The debate among the historians of the Israelite people over the mode of establishment in the land favors the enumeration of tribes above every other aspect of the text. The almost exclusive interest in this theme imposes, as a code, an attitude toward the text that blinds the historian to its documentary richness, visible as soon as the conception of history is enlarged to include the imagination. This broadening is precisely what the anthropological code will accomplish. Thus the historian who favors chapter 5 as a historical source will avoid interpreting the whole of the text; he/she will select from it what his/her code prescribes; moreover, the differences between the two versions will be explained, if need be, by the literary code. In other words, the historian will avoid accounting for both texts insofar as they are *texts,* in order to construct, *on the basis of* the texts, a referent then put forward as an argument *against* the texts. This circularity is perhaps inevitable in historical research; viewed from the perspective that concerns us here, the fact remains that it leads to an act of censorship biased against the less collective themes other codes are liable to address. Thus, the historical code, which could be powerful if it admitted its necessarily biased character, creative if it recognized its anachronisms, and fruitful if it widened its too narrow domain, in practice often destroys semantic aspects of the texts whose importance is undeniable. When it is employed connotatively to cloak the anachronistic moral code with the authority of history, it becomes clearly repressive.

·2·

THE THEOLOGICAL CODE

The theological code interprets the texts as testimonies of specific religious feelings that characterized the Judaic religion at its beginnings. This theme is not unrelated to that of the war of conquest, which is characteristic of the preceding code. The motivation underlying the great "conquest" was constructed as religious. Deborah's patriotism, so often praised, was inspired by her commitment to the Covenant with Yahweh. This religion, exceptional to the region of Canaan and on its way to becoming monotheistic, helped the Hebrews create their identity and distinguish themselves from the sedentary peoples. At the same time, the tendency to assimilate was strong. The book of Judges follows the circular movement that results from these two opposing tendencies. First, the Hebrews assimilate, commit "evil in the sight of the Lord" (2:11). The evil in question is defined thus: "And they forsook the Lord, and served Baal and the Ashtaroth" (2:13). Next, to punish them for their infidelity, Yahweh "sells" them "into the hand of" the enemy, who oppresses them for twenty or forty years. Then, a deliverer-judge who leads the sacred war is given to them. After the victory, they return to their evil ways. The episode of Deborah fits into this scheme.

The study of this religious, or religio-nationalist, background functions as a code when it is called upon to structure the meaning of the texts. For example, Deborah's enthusiasm is interpreted as originating from her religious commitment; the song states this connection much more explicitly than the narrative. The comparison between Yahwism and the Canaanite religion emphasizes this enthusiasm. Certain interpreters ascribe a moral value to the differences that leads them to expunge the similarities discovered by others, something that allows us to see how two codes mutually influence each other.

It is surprising to observe that the theological code seems capable of impeding its own progress when it leads to the suppression of the theological difference between the two versions, which remains obvious nevertheless. We will try to understand how an underlying code makes use of the theological code in order to remain unperceived. Also, the theological code leads the interpreter to enhance the religious aspect, and this bias will again prove to be restrictive, a form of censorship.

It is important to understand Deborah's religious motivation and the way she draws her persuasive force from it. We see this power in both versions. In the first, she uses it to push Barak to overcome his terror before the superior strength of the enemy. She invokes the will of Yahweh at the moment of preparation (4:7). The importance and the image of Yahweh are radically different in the song, where practically *everything* is identified with or dedicated to Yahweh: the commitment of the participating tribes, the battle itself, nature, the song, the act of Jael, the anxiety of Sisera's mother. The song is penetrated with religious feeling; while it is a means of political persuasion in 4, Deborah makes it the *raison d'être* of the entire community in 5. If the prose version is more epic, the lyric song places its accents elsewhere.

For the moment two points are worth noting:

1. The theological code can serve to bring out the differences between the two versions.
2. The religious code is at work in the texts themselves. The change in register between 4 and 5 is at least partially due to the more profoundly religious code by which the poetess expresses herself.

It is important to distinguish these two points. For the first, we will have to examine to what degree the possibilities of the theological code are effectively exploited. The second aspect identifies a first group-code. We must not forget that Deborah is fully integrated into a group—the group of Israelite believers, of faithful Yahwists—whose language she speaks. This language seems less predominant in the words of the epic narrator.

The Use of the Theological Code

Let us begin our examination where we left off in the last chapter, with the analysis of a combination of codes. Popular commentary provides a revealing example. Gore et al. (1928:204) insist upon Deborah's religious inspiration. Here is how the theological code is led to justify, that is, to relativize, an implicit moral code judged to be too restrictive:

> The Song is inspired throughout by intense religious patriotism. . . .
> This is the standard by which the tribes are condemned who failed to
> answer the call to arms . . . ; and this is the standard by which Jael is
> accounted blessed for her murder of Sisera, in which the writer sees
> only a glorious act of patriotism in contrast to the cowardly neutrality
> of Meroz, and regards Jael as the instrument of Divine vengeance
> upon her people's foe.

The underlying contradiction in this passage arises out of the clash of two codes, each bound by a different loyalty; the one exhorts us to praise Jael along with Deborah; the other, to condemn her. The theological code prevails here, but the other code is only momentarily anesthetized; its validity is at the same time acknowledged, as shown by the insistence upon the norm in force as only one of a number of possible norms.

The comparison between Yahwism and the polytheistic cults of the Canaanites is not always so positively understood. Cundall (1968:87) describes Deborah's god in this way: "The Lord was often depicted as the God of the thunderstorm, moving in awful splendor and power to the help of his people," and puts this cosmic image of Yahweh on the same level as Baal: "the Israelites did not have a monopoly on this conception . . . the Canaanites looked upon Baal in much the same way. He was the storm-god, the rider upon the clouds." Indeed, the god of chapter 5 represents a hybrid image combining the god of war of chapter 4, resembling the Germanic Wodan, and the cosmic god reminiscent of the Germanic Donar—he who moves the storms according to the will of the faithful. It is hardly astonishing that two such terrifying images should be integrated into a single vision of a god who is lord of human dangers and prodigious catastrophes.

The same image, interpreted by means of the same code, gives rise to a completely different interpretation in Gore et al. (1928:204): "The conception of God . . . the Warrior-god of battles, [was] a conception which, however imperfect, was vastly higher than the idea of God held by the Palestinian tribes, which reduced Jehovah to the level of the gods of the soil, the agricultural Baalim of the Canaanites." It is all too clear, however, that the theological code serves to conceal a different, more shameful code, one that joins an evolutionist perspective to a monotheistic commitment in a positive evaluation of war. This evaluation elevates the god of war above the peaceful gods of agriculture. What stands out here is the difference between the theological (meta-)code and the religious code, tied respectively to the scientific and the personal perspective. In the present case, the religious code compels the interpreter to oppose the warrior god to the gods of agriculture. What determines the selection of this particular opposition? Analysis of the commentary reveals a thought process founded upon two archetypal structures characteristic of our culture. First, the binary opposition that accompanies any hierarchy of values is a fundamental code whose tenacity is well known. White (1972) gives an excellent analysis of the use of the particular form of that code involved here. It serves to authenticate the cultural conception of oneself, difficult to justify, by means of the devaluation of another. The technique is called "ostensive self-definition by negation." It is frequently resorted to at moments of cultural uncertainty and is therefore the index of a profound feeling of insecurity. White (1972:5) clarifies how the technique becomes a restrictive code:

> They [the concepts] are treated neither as provisional designators, that is, as hypotheses for directing further inquiry into specific areas of human experience, nor as fictions with limited heuristic utility for generating possible ways of conceiving the human world. They are, rather, complexes of symbols, the referents of which shift and change in response to the changing patterns of human behavior which they are meant to sustain.

The key concept of this code, according to White, is that of the *savage*, of the *primitive*, often invoked in reference to the song.

Less obvious here, but just as influential, is a second code that I call *figurative*, which almost irresistibly leads the interpreter to structure semes in a figure of comparison, where the opposition is installed within a network of contiguity and similarity. The deities at stake are here considered in the opposition *high-low* based on two different senses of these words. On the one hand, the opposition is situated in the physical comparant of the image (cloud-soil). In other words, it is metonymically motivated (Genette 1972:41–63). On the other hand, it is situated in the compared, the appended moral values (elevated = more evolved; low = primitive). Then it is projected, in both senses, upon the two peoples. The mechanism at work can be represented as a "semiotic square" (Greimas 1970:141ff.), which assumes in the present study a very different function from the more positivist one it has in traditional semiotic discourse (fig. 1). There it is intended to represent the structure of objective semantic domains; here it is the schematization of an ideologeme; not only its content, but also its "abstract" structure is considered ideological. It is meant to analyze the structuration of modern semantics. This semantics represses, by virtue of its "scientific" structure, aspects of the text that lend themselves to interpretation as soon as the binary optic is abandoned. The mediating position I confer upon the "semantic square" makes it possible to see the close connections between the different aspects of a code—its *configuration*, White would say. The figure represents one of the basic modes of Western ethnocentric thought. It should be mentioned in passing that the Baal of storms has disappeared from the scene—and for good reasons.

The analysis shows how an attitude, a specific ideology entrusted with protecting the interest of its adherents, takes on the bearing of a code. Indeed, the mechanism biases the interpretation in so "natural" a fashion that the latter goes almost unperceived. It is not presented as interpretation: no sign of the interpretive act is present in the discourse— neither the verb "signify" nor any synonym, nor any equivalent of "understand," nor even a reference to a detail of the text upon which an

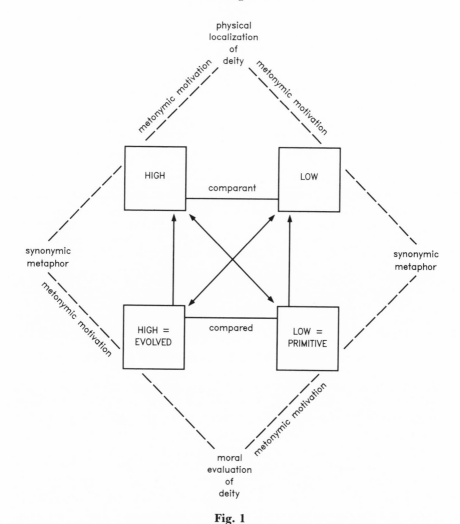

Fig. 1

interpretation could possibly be based. The interpretive act thus manages to escape contradiction and can all the more effectively direct the rest of the commentary.

At this point we begin to understand that the difference between the two versions has to be mitigated. The opposition between the Yahwists and the Baalists, which is the whole point of the religious conviction being expressed in the commentary, must be enhanced at the expense, on the one hand, of the similarity between the two religions, and, on the other, of the difference between the two images of Yahweh in 4 and 5. One group is formed by assimilating two other groups—that of the epic narrator and that of the lyric poetess—and by casting off another group—that of the adherents of a pantheistic religion.

Richter's study (1963) again provides a characteristic example of the type of "learned" reasoning that sanctions the elimination of difference. The "problems," according to Richter (69), begin at verse 5:4, the representation of the theophany. A comparison with Ps. 68:8–10 is drawn to reassure readers who may be anxious about the differences. There, too, the name of Yahweh is the first indication of the presence of the god. The difference that remains is minimized, and the complements of the song are condemned (1963:70):

> . . . das *pedantische* "Wolken troffen Wassers." Das Nebeneinander von Erde und Himmel mit je typischen Bewegungen *beinhalten im Grunde alles;* die folgenden Angaben über Wolken und Berge fügen nichts neues hinzu, sondern differenzieren *schulmeisterlich,* wobei sie die universal *gemeinte,* da die Pole angebende, Aussäge über Erde und Himmel *in der Tendenz beschränkt.*

> . . . the *pedantic* "the clouds poured forth water." The juxtaposition of earth and sky with their typical movements *contains basically all;* the following complements of clouds and the mountains add nothing new at all, but differentiate *pedantically,* limiting the reach of the declaration about the earth and the sky, the *intention* of which was to express the universal by indicating its poles. (My italics)

We recognize the procedure: from an interpretation guided by a personal evaluation of what "contains all" and of what, consequently, can be considered superfluous, the critic goes on to attribute to the text an intention with respect to which other fragments can be rejected. He sacrifices all that differentiates this text from the other, all that is characteristic of this particular representation of the theophany, in brief, the entire theological import of the text. This was a necessary sacrifice: it is precisely the rejected details that draw the parallel with the Canaanite religion. Others (Taylor 1982) interpret this parallel as at least polemic, or ironic. The solution is perhaps a little too easy, but even so, slightly further from censorship. The word "pedantic" is repeated several times in the rest of Richter's commentary, and the tone of irritation, truly exceptional in this rather dry discourse, is poorly concealed. It only shows us all the more clearly that we are faced with symptoms of an undisclosed condition, a bias barely repressed.

The procedure opens up the theological code to other codes, and from theological interpretation to moral interpretation is only a small step, based on the metaphoric "translations" we have seen at work. Once this connection is established (phase 1), the way is clear for other moral and consequently anachronistic judgments (phase 2). Gore et al. continue (206):

[phase 1]   Not only was the religion of Canaan a fertility cult, but whether it was the highly developed pantheon of the city-states or the primitive Baal of the local shrine, its polytheistic character made nonsense of any standards of morality. . . .

[phase 2]   It was a degradation of worship to identify it with sexual intercourse with religious prostitutes, it was deadly peril to morality to pay homage to a variety of deities among whom moral standards were non-existent.

Sexuality is here introduced through two doorways: the cult of fertility indeed venerated the feminine principle as the primary repository of fertility, but even polytheism itself, devoted to plurality, seems to trouble the modern Christian commentator devoted to singularity—to monogamy just as much as to monotheism. For him, the two go hand in hand; an equivalence that should not be taken for granted for the Israelite still only in the process of becoming monotheistic, and remaining (under certain conditions, it is true) polygamous. The ideologeme (or the ideological isotopy; see Jameson 1981) that results from this equation can be represented in fig. 2. What characterizes this ideologeme is an interpretive procedure in two stages: first, plurality is correlated with the absence of morality; next, religious plurality with sexual plurality. The scheme is found in numerous commentaries as well as in biblical texts, often in the form of the metaphor [infidelity to Yahweh ≃ prostitution]. We encounter it in the frequent formula "they . . . served Baal and the Ashtaroth" (2:13), already cited. Baal, here, is presented in the singular, even though it can be interpreted as a generic name for the male Canaanite gods. The word signifies /master/ or /husband/, an interesting equivalence. The Ashtaroth are goddesses. The word is in the plural form. Thus the formula expresses in miniature the central concern at stake. To serve *a number of Ashtaroth* must be twice as bad as serving *a single Baal*. The scheme of the ideologeme is nevertheless not general, and, significantly, there is not the least trace of it in the song.

The theological code is thus capable of interpreting the differences between the two versions, but in practice its focus lies elsewhere. This is because between the theological (meta-)code and the religious code of the commentators there is no clear border but a wavering line, and the moral code is always free to cross that line and establish its presence. This explains the fact that the majority of commentators I consulted subordinate the theological code to the historical code and make much more of the problem of Jabin and the tribes than of the theological difference, which they treat as accessory.

The difference, however, is considerable and deserves to be pointed out. It shows just how far the theological code can go when it is not frustrated in its purposes by the historical code; furthermore, the theo-

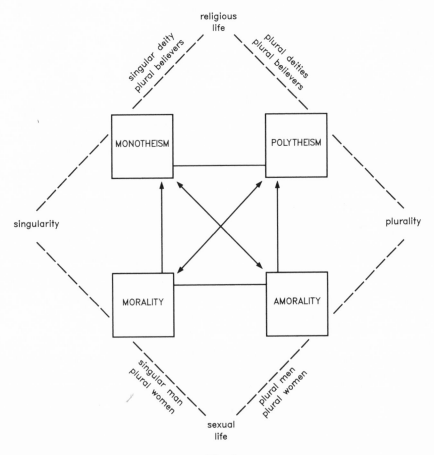

religious
life

singular deity
plural believers

plural deities
plural believers

MONOTHEISM   POLYTHEISM

singularity   plurality

MORALITY   AMORALITY

singular man
plural women

plural men
plural women

sexual
life

Fig. 2

logical theme is inextricably tied to the anthropological thematic network, and, as we shall see later, it is not without relevance for the delim-
itation and the integration of the gender codes. We must take the analysis still further.

Religious Codes

The theological code that seeks to interpret the religious theme of both
texts must consider the texts as they are. Contrary to the historical-
critical code, the point of departure here will be the "facts" concerning
the present state of the texts: two versions, one older than the other,
autonomous and perhaps related.

We have seen how, in chapter 4, the image of the warrior god is functionally evoked to persuade Barak to vanquish his fear before the superiority of the enemy, which is a superiority of civilization: "for he had nine hundred chariots of iron; and twenty years he mightily oppressed . . ." (4:3). Nine hundred chariots of iron constitute a striking force clearly superior to the ten thousand men that Barak appears able to recruit. This means that the technological advantage, due to what is considered a more sophisticated level of civilization, will have to be compensated for at another level. Deborah implicitly suggests the means: "And I will draw towards you by the river Kishon Sisera, the commander of Jabin's army, with all his chariots and his multitude; and I will deliver him into your hand" (4:7). Against chariots of iron, she offers the torrent of Kishon, thus defying the opposition between nature and culture. There is nothing theological about the strategy. Consequently Barak does not react according to that code. If he obeys despite his fear, it is because Deborah promises to march with him.

When the time comes the prophetess announces to Barak that Yahweh has chosen his day: "Up; for this is the day in which the Lord has delivered Sisera into your hand: has not the Lord gone out before you?" (4:14). Once again, Yahweh is invoked in order to persuade, but the image is more concrete than it was in verse 6 ("Has not the Lord God of Israel commanded . . . ?"). In Deborah's second, and equally rhetorical, speech, it is possible to see the appearance of a sign, if not an epiphany in embryo, that is not otherwise elaborated. The image implicit in "gone out" is ambiguous. Either, still rhetorical, it identifies Yahweh with his spokeswoman, meaning simply that the prophetess will go with Barak if he marches on that day, or it is to be read in the light of the song, and Yahweh will then have assumed the concrete form of a cloud. Murray (1979) suggests the presence here of a double code: that of Barak, who interprets Deborah as the representative of Yahweh, and that of Deborah, who conceives of Yahweh in terms both more concrete and more powerful. The question is significant, for we glimpse here the possibility of a play (ironic, Murray would say) between two different codes, both of them religious, which the theological code is able to show interacting. On the whole, however, the narrative of chapter 4, with the exception of 4:14, represents a rather abstract warrior god, a moral support rather than an active character, and entirely bound, for Barak, to the person of Deborah.

In the song, the god is omnipresent, and the opposition set up by the prophetess between the chariots of iron, sign of a more evolved civilization, and the forces of nature, sign of a more integrated religion, becomes vital. It works at two levels now: at the strategic level, where it explains the function of the torrent that will render the chariots useless, and at the theological level, where the forces of nature join to support— or to become—Yahweh. That *to support* comes to be equivalent to *to become* characterizes the religion of the poetess. The third stanza especially presents elements of this pantheist theology. The verb "go out" with Yahweh as subject, the only verb that recurs in the epic narrative, introduces a series of verbs descriptive of action on the cosmic scale in which all the elements participate. The natural catastrophe that makes the Kishon overflow its banks leaves the chariots of Sisera stuck in the mud. Immobilized, the enemy immediately loses the advantage of his civilization. Fear is absent from this version, which attributes the storm to the intervention of the deity whose power is celebrated. The "natural" explanation of the storm, which might find its cause in the volatile atmospheric conditions of the mountainous countries in spring, is not thereby refuted, but ignored or integrated.

The evocation of the cosmos is resumed later, toward the end of the evaluation of the tribes. Here, the image is slightly different: "From heaven the stars fought; in their courses they fought against Sisera. The river of Kishon swept them away, that ancient river, the river Kishon" (5:20–21). The commentator who has diverted the theological code toward the moral code by means of the synonymic metaphor /high-elevated/, /low-primitive/, is at a loss for what to do with this image. Consequently, he does not comment on it. Richter, who had explained verse 4 to his satisfaction, suggests that a new text begins at verse 6 (1963:86): "da V.6. neue, der Gottestat diametral entgegengesetzte Angaben bringen" (verse 6 here brings new indications, which are diametrically opposed to the divine intervention). Thus he strips verse 20 of all theological value. He continues: "und wird nirgends, auch nicht in V.20, wieder aufgenommen, denn der Kamp der Sterne entspricht sicher einer anderen, sehr alten Auffassung" (and [the divine act] is nowhere restated, not even in verse 20, since the combat of the stars originates surely from another, very old conception).

We can invert this argument, and, rather than affirm the customary monotheistic Yahwism to be solely applicable, begin with this "other, very old conception," which would be equally basic to the theophany of verse 4. No element of this evocation would then be "pedantic" or "superfluous." It appears difficult to accept this point of view. Many commentators insist upon the strangeness of the image. Equating the cosmos with the cause of Yahweh, they pronounce his *absence* in the song. If his omnipresence is there affirmed, his name, the name that would individualize him, is absent. Soggin (1981:95) writes: "In it [the description of the battle] the figure of the God of Israel seems strangely to be absent." This incomprehension of the particular theology of the song is easy to explain. The stars evoked here are compared with those of Canaanite theology, where they are the sources of rain (Boling 1975:113). Deborah's vision is indeed a highly specific blending of Yahwist and Canaanite elements, in which above all the profound unity between Yahweh, nature, and the Hebrew people predominates. This is the religious feeling before the disenchantment that comes in the wake of the technological mastering of the cosmos. The mixture is at the same time the indication of a profound difference from the Canaanite civilization. The latter is more advanced and by this fact has lost its unity with nature. In a sense, Deborah shows herself more Baalist than the Baalists, which raises problems for the commentator more Catholic than the pope. For the believer who conceives of history as a dynamic form of evolution, always in progress, in which the Hebrew people have a stable identity, there is more than one paradox here. Outside of this evolutionist bias, however, Deborah can be viewed here as the advocate of an integrative religion, archaic or not, in which unity prevails over "progress," alienating because it is inharmonious and destabilizing.

We have seen that the cosmic aspect of this evocation practically disappears in the more recent version of the prose narrative. At the same time, the impact of Yawheh has clearly diminished. Here the Septuagint intervenes. Verse 4:8—"And Barak said to her, if you go with me, then I will go; but if you will not go with me, then I will not go!"—in which Barak expresses his desperate need for Deborah's support, is completed in the Greek version by "une curieuse phrase qui aurait pu faire partie du texte primitif" (a curious sentence which could have belonged to the primitive text) (Dhorme 1956:729): "Car je ne sais pas le jour dans lequel l'Ange du Seigneur fera bon voyage avec moi" (For I do not know the day on which the Angel of the Lord will make good journey with me). According to Dhorme, the "omission" of this line in the Hebrew text could be due to the error called *homeoteleuton*, provoked by the repetition of the ending "with me." What we have here is an example of the shifting of the philological code into the theological code. If the interpretation is not refutable (non-falsifiability constituting the central problem of this discipline), there is no good reason why we should not invert the argument. It is not, then, the suppression of the line in the Hebrew copy that must be explained, but its addition in the Greek text, in which the tendency to add theological elements is well known. (See Von Rad 1965:119–25 on the conception of the "day of the lord.") The conclusion, in the present case, will differ depending on whether the theological code is manipulated in open and unrestricted fashion, or contrariwise, as an instrument of closure. An open application will address and acknowledge the evidence of the reduced importance of the god in the narrative as compared to the song. It will explain the Greek supplement as the effect of a restriction determined by the following argument: /The more there is of Yahweh in 4, the fewer differences there are between 4 and 5, and the better it is/. This argument in turn is substantiated by the competition between Deborah and Yahweh that is the consequence of the alteration. If one explained it in this way, the theological code could avoid fusing with the religious code of the Septuagint. In a closed application, on the other hand, the code will not escape that fusion.

Another bias, which we will call gendered, joins that belonging to the Septuagint. I explain it thus: the fact that Barak's dependence upon Deborah is considered shameful—and the response attributed to Deborah confirms this judgment—could have led the Septuagint to introduce a theological argument at precisely this point in the text. The interpreter who too quickly accepts the primacy here of the Greek text closes the theological code to the differences between the two versions. The code then changes alliance: from the opposition Yahwist-Baalist, the code is surreptitiously realigned along the opposition men-women, while still ostensibly remaining centered on the theme of Yahwism.

Let us summarize the results of the open application of the theological code. In the two texts, the image of Yahweh is differentiated as in fig. 3. Two observations are pertinent here. First, it is not possible to oppose the two images term by term. There are common traits (for example, warrior) and antithetical traits (abstract-concrete), but also *nonopposed differentials*. The principal feature in which difference takes precedence over opposition is the numerical seme. If the image is clearly singular in the narrative, in accordance with monotheism, it is simultaneously singular and plural in the song, or rather, the category is irrelevant there. The plural cosmic forces *are* the singular Yahweh, and in place of a number, what is represented is the infinite localization of his presence throughout the universe. Deborah the poetess thus breaks out of the frame of the ideologeme sketched in fig. 2, and with her she takes her god, who is, we might say, singular and plural at the same time. This brings me to a second observation. If we maintain that the narrative has used the song as a source, or that the words originate from a common source, the repetition of the verbal form *go out* constitutes an interesting case of *intertextuality* (Kristeva 1968:47; 1974:59–60): the citation of a word or phrase whose displacement radically changes its meaning. But there is more to it than that. Given the profound difference between the two images, which are the products of radically different modes or *discourses*, we can at the same time speak here of *interdiscursivity* (Moser 1981).

To Jakobson's typology (1971:261), which distinguishes three kinds of translation, intralinguistic, interlinguistic, and intersemiotic, Moser (1981:6) adds interdiscursive translation, which he defines as follows (1981:14):

> It consists in the carrying over of discourse elements from one type of discourse to another. The discourse elements can be of quite different nature: verbal features, stylistic features, modes of predication, concepts, objects, methods, pragmatic features, institutional connections.

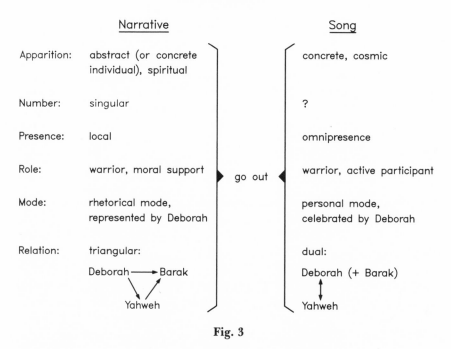

Fig. 3

The words "go out," which constitute a verbal element of a concrete vocabulary, are transferred to the epic discourse to assume there a different meaning, affected by the surrounding discourse into which it has been set. In the song, Yahweh was its subject, and the addressee of the sentence as well as of the action was, again, Yahweh. His action, as well as the nonutilitarian, personal discourse that celebrates it, thereby becomes absolute. In the narrative, the subject Yahweh becomes the *object* of the discourse, the absentee who is the "third person," excluded from the situation of enunciation (Benveniste 1966). His action thereby loses its concrete and absolute character; it is of direct and practical benefit to the masculine figure who is the addressee of the discourse, a discourse now become utilitarian and rhetorical. It would be a mistake, however, to connect interdiscursivity exclusively to a polemical or ironic intention. Here, it carries out an *imperialist* function: the second discourse *monopolizes* the word, exploits it for its own advantage, "proves its innocence" in a way, which is to say, expurgates it of connotations dangerous to the new theology henceforth in effect.

The transformation this interdiscursivity works in the position of Barak is revealing. Deborah's speech, more concrete, personal, and exclamatory in the song than it is when embedded in the epic discourse, is addressed directly to Yahweh. The ensuing relation demonstrates the marginality of Barak: addressee of Deborah's discourse on Yahweh in the narrative, he is practically irrelevant in the song, where the addressee is no less than Yahweh himself. This displacement, from 5 to 4, of the masculine character from periphery to center reflects the importance attached to history on the individual level in both versions. An actantial analysis would lay bare the double structure of the narrative, in which the couple Barak-Sisera vies with that of Deborah-Jael to attain the stature of actantial subject. Yahweh is there no more than adjuvant. In the song he is, if not subject, at least addressee, and Barak has no function at all.

A comparison of the way the historical and theological codes function reveals similarities and differences. Both are led to emphasize one of the two versions at the expense of the other. Both are easily linked to the parasitic moral code, which, in the one case as much as in the other, diminishes the autonomy of the feminine characters. Although both are important for an understanding of the background of the two texts, the theological code has a more significant potential for differentiation. Unfortunately, the intimate bond between the theological meta-code and the personal religious code creates an additional problem. It leads many an interpreter to close off the code in all directions except that proper to the religious institution, even if it means leaving unaddressed the differences due to the different religous affiliations of the two interlocutors, colored as well by sexual differentiation. This censorship is not inherent in the theological code—we will see it in force elsewhere—and a critical analysis of its functioning seems vital to achieving a truly differential theological interpretation.

An examination of the religious codes of the texts brings the crucial differences to the fore. Conducted carefully, it will enable us to understand what happened in the course of the evolution of the Judeo-Christian religion at its beginnings. The relations of reciprocal dependence between religion and politics on the one hand, and between religion and sexual ideology on the other, deserve to be integrated into the knowledge of our cultural past. It is only when we accept the religious codes of each of the two texts that we can measure the difference not only between them but between two historical phases as well, or between two cultural communities. The acceptance of this difference creates a semiotic freedom that can only be enriching.

·3·

THE ANTHROPOLOGICAL CODE

Anthropology, in the broadest sense, is interested in the cultural life of different human societies. Related to several disciplines, it is distinguished by its perspective, which is comprehensive, and by its methods, empathic observation being the most characteristic (see Boon 1982; Honigmann 1963; Pelto 1970). If historians seek to reconstruct the evolution of the Israelite people from scattered seminomadic tribes to Judaic kingdom, anthropologists examine their way of life, reconstructing fragments of it from texts and other sources. Their interests are multiple, and it follows that their relation to the text varies depending on the problem to be resolved. For the examination of codes that we are pursuing, three anthropological aspects turn out to be extremely important: the concept of *judge;* certain aspects of the practical way of life (the ethnographic context); and the question of oral tradition.

The anthropological perspective functions as code when questions concerning the cultural life of Hebraic society, as it is represented in the texts, serve as the directing theme for interpretation. The concept of judge, whose importance is obvious, sheds light on the political, judicial, social, and military structure of the community. The attitude of the interpreter toward this problematic concept will be decisive for his/her appreciation of the represented actions of different characters. Other aspects of tribal life serve to structure both versions of the story. The chariots of iron have already been dealt with, given their importance for the religious vision and for the outcome of the battle. The opposition between valley and mountain is related. But the story of Jael is difficult to understand without precise knowledge of the tribes' seminomadic way of life. The consequences of such a life for the division of labor between the sexes are significant for the interpretation. Details of the story, from the milk offered to Sisera and the way in which Jael invites the leader into her tent, up to the embroidered scarf evoked in the last stanza, serve as signifying elements in the representation of the diegesis, which cannot be understood without them. The anthropological code will prove to be extremely powerful; without it, it would become difficult to construct a comprehensive and differential thematic network embracing both texts.

The anthropology of orality, a fairly autonomous branch that has recently experienced a certain revival (Finnegan 1977; Goody and Watt 1968; Ong 1977, 1982), studies the fundamental implications that the evolution of an oral culture into a generally literate society has had for thought and culture in general, and for literature in particular (Zumthor 1982). The perspective of orality functions as code when features of the text are interpreted in its light. We are less concerned, this time, with motifs representing aspects of history, than with formal, stylistic, or compositional aspects of history, than with formal, stylistic, or compositional aspects whose thematic repercussions are no less considerable. The three distinct functions of the anthropological code are all equally valuable for an elucidation of the difference between 4 and 5.

The Concept of Judge

The concept of judge, which has given the book its title, is problematic in several respects. The signification of the root *špt* is acknowledged to be obscure. The problem typifies the circularity inherent in the enterprise of interpretation: the unique source available for the concept's interpretation is the very book that requires interpretation by means of this concept. And even this book provides only the most sparing information; only chapter 4 goes beyond the simple mention of the root. The only character-judge who does something beyond killing enemies is Deborah. The manner in which the anthropological discourse arrives at a decision on the function of the judge and on the character of Deborah betrays the suppression of a conflict. Apparently Deborah is a troubling case. Many interpreters ignore Deborah the judge; others hasten to assert that she was not a judge at all. One of these is Soggin (1981:64), who declares without any justification whatsoever: "It should also be noted that the 'judgeship' of Deborah seems to have been used for reckoning time." He challenges the reality of the function of the poetess. Those who take her status as judge seriously are still left with two options: either she is a judge, but Barak alone leads the battle or even shares Deborah's function; or she belongs, along with Barak, to those judges who are not truly judges but "deliverers," a very different, temporary function, which would have been assimilated to the first by our friend the redactor.

Following in the tradition of Richter, Mayes (1974) distinguishes those judges properly called "deliverers." The argument behind the distinction should be considered in detail; it has its consequences. The primary source is constituted by the "list of judges": the designation, in 10:1–5 and 12:7–15, of six men of whom it is said that they "judged"—the root *špt*—Israel. The story of Jephthah is inserted between the two "parts" of the list, but it is clear that Judg. 10:1–5; 12:7–15 originally formed a connected list. Its present broken state resulted from the fact that Jephthah the Gileadite was not only numbered among these judges but was also the subject of a tradition portraying him as a deliverer in the manner of the other deliverers such as Gideon and Samson. (Mayes 1974:55–56)

A first interpretive decision is thus presented as axiomatic. If we still leave open the possibility that the deliverers could have been included in this list, its unity is not questioned. The conspicuous interruption by the story of Jephthah is generally noted; as the unity of the list is considered incontestable, the intercalation is systematically explained by the "double" status of the character who, exceptionally and as if by chance, is *both* judge *and* deliverer.

The unity of the list is affirmed with such assurance because of its literary form. It is described as follows (Mayes 1974:59):

1 each judge is linked to his predecessor by the words "after him;"
2 of each judge it is said that the "judged Israel . . . years;"
3 of each judge it is said that he "died . . . and was buried at."

This formal scheme serves as an argument for the possible inclusion of a number of deliverers in the list. The list, in its form and unity, acts then as a code. But what if the list consisted simply of two fragments of a longer list, or of two independent lists? The question is not even raised.

The root *špṭ* replaces or summarizes, according to Mayes, the activities of these figures, activities that, in the case of the deliverers, are related in detail. If their activities went beyond the judiciary domain, their exploits would certainly have been retained. The evidence, again, is the case of Jephthah:

In fact, it is precisely the appearance of Jephthah both in the list of those who "judged" Israel and among the deliverers which would lead us to the conclusion that the activities of those men who are said to have judged Israel belonged in the legal sphere; they were judges, and it was as such that they were remembered in the tradition. Had they been deliverers there would have been traditions telling of their exploits as there are of Jephthah and the other deliverers. (58)

The repetition signals the circularity of the argument. In fact, it is not so obvious, as is here suggested, that Jephthah is mentioned twice. He is *in* the list, not with the schematic formula but with a story *in place of the formula*. This sheds light on the function of the formula itself, which I will return to shortly.

Besides the unity of the list and its codified form, the root *špṭ* is examined. If it seems to summarize the activities of the judges of the list, it also appears in other cases, notably signifying the role of certain deliverers.

Given the preestablished distinction, the root cannot have the same meaning in both cases. The argument here does not proceed beyond the simple repetition of the word *unlikely:* "because the *reason* for the names of these men having been preserved is to be found in the records about them as charismatic deliverers, it is unlikely that the root [*špṭ*], when used in connection with them, has the same connotation as it has when applied to the members of the list" (58; my italics). We recognize, in the word *reason,* an appeal to intention that constitutes a preliminary interpretive act whose result is then used as a code. But the semantic counterargument is acknowledged to be quite formidable; hence the rest of the sentence, which refutes it with the following all-purpose argument: "or if it has the same connotation then the application of the root to the charismatic deliverers does not correspond with their historical activities, but should be seen rather as the work of the editor of these traditions" (58). Patiently, the critic dismisses all possible refutations, always on the basis of his *a priori* decision. The case that poses a problem, Jephthah, is the exception that proves the rule. This figure presents a revealing case indeed. He is called upon for assistance in wartime, and he refuses the position of leader of the army (*qāṣîn*) to demand that of leader of the people (*rō'š*). Such a request could well be explained by the permanence of the second function, as opposed to the first. The root *špṭ* seems to indicate a permanent function, since the "reign" of each member of the list is cited, and brought to a close by the death of the official.

Since the argument leading to the distinction between *Richter* (judge) and *Retter* (deliverer) does not escape from the situation of aporia where the preliminary interpretive act had confined it in the first place (see also Gooding 1982), let us try another approach. The book of Judges consists of three types of discourse: the *narration* of spectacular exploits directed by a leader; the *enumeration* of state officials, the *šōpeṭîm;* and the *narration* of spectacular events not directed by a leader. To begin with the last: chapters 17–21 are generally considered out of place, because they represent what happens precisely when there is no leader. This is why the period of the judges leads to the transition, via Samuel, to the kingdom. The discourse of 17–21 implies therefore, let us say, a condemnation of chaos. The lists enumerate the lifelong bureaucratic functions, devoid of exploits, to which the officials are summoned by Yahweh after the sin of religious chaos. The narration of directed events relates the brilliant exploits that intervene, sporadically, in that dark chaos. Like the officials, the heroic figures are also summoned to their task by Yahweh. The difference seems to inhere less in the functions of the official and of the hero than in the state of the land over which they preside: a state of sin in the first case—internal chaos; a state of oppression in the second—external chaos. In other words, the figure of the *šōpeṭ* has the same function, but the situation he/she is called upon to remedy is different.

This distinction explains the absence of military exploits for the figures on the list: there was no need for such exploits at that time. The last discourse represents the inevitable chaos that ensues when no one leads the people: neither peace nor war, but a chaos within the land, which slaughters just as many but brings honor to no one.

The notion of *chaos* is thus central to this discussion. Whether the chaos be caused externally or internally, the central root of the book can only signify the act of remedying: /to put back in order/, /to repair/. The difference lies not in the ambiguity of the verb but in that of its object. The problem is comparable to that raised by the notion of *mimesis*, de- rived, in the Western aesthetic tradition, from the verb *mimeisthai* in Aristotle's *Poetics* (Dupont-Roc and Lallot 1980; Bal 1982). The object of this verb can be *at the same time* the thing represented and the result of this representation; only the modern mind, which abhors ambiguity, felt the need to choose between the two possibilities. Analytic thought thus stripped the notion of its potential semantic value, inaugurating the long tradition that we know, in which the aesthetic of imitation (mimetic in the falsely narrow sense) is incompatible with the aesthetic of creation. This tradition rests at least in part upon an anachronistic interpretation of the Greek verb, rendered unambiguous. The myth of *Richter* versus *Retter* is based on an analogous act of definition.

The most significant discursive detail is the juxtaposition, in scholarly discourse, of the argument and its fragile base, and the facts liable to refute it. Thus some have not failed to notice the probable parallel be- tween *šōpeṭ* and the Carthaginian *sufetes,* a function designated by the same root. This was a governmental office in force during the periods when there was no hereditary monarchy (Mayes 1977:321). The func- tion was not limited to the judiciary domain that it encompassed; it included a more general directive function. We know that political sys- tems, let us say, prior to the theories of Montesquieu, did not generally distinguish between the various domains of powers in which authority was exercised. In addition, cases of "charismatic" persons capable of monopolizing power in different spheres are still numerous in the mod- ern period. As late as 1876, the Americans came up against the synthetic power of the Indian chief Sitting Bull, who was able to win the battle of Little Bighorn thanks to the combination of his talents as strategist, religious leader, administrator, physician, and confidant. Unable to con- ceive the possibility of such a synthesis, the Americans were routed. Still more recently, de Gaulle was able, after the war, to find himself invested with an exorbitant political power because he had distinguished himself as a war hero, as a "deliverer." Conversely, the military blunders of Leopold of Belgium cost him his political position. The charisma at- tached to "deliverers" in wartime was largely responsible in these cases.

What does this discussion have to do with chapters 4 and 5? Given the facility with which the case of Deborah, so spectacularly problematic, is suppressed, I suspect that the political theory of the "deliverer," crudely elaborated as it is, has a direct bearing upon it. For those who subscribe to the theory of the list, Deborah is not a judge, because she does not figure in it. If she holds the office of *špṭ* under the "palm tree of Deborah," Richter (1963:42) considers the verse a corruption and confers upon the character only the status of prophetess. On the other hand, she cannot be an autonomous "deliverer," because she herself assigns this temporary function to Barak. Curiously enough, in the discussion her case is systematically referred to as "Deborah-Barak"; there is good reason for this, provided that one presupposes the separation of judge and deliverer. The critics who advance this circular argument draw from her case a double-edged weapon: Deborah becomes less powerful and a factor less troubling for the theory.

I would suggest beginning from the opposite point of view. Reversing the argument, let us suppose for a moment that the text in which the function is more explicitly defined is the more reliable source. It would be necessary, then, to begin with the case of Deborah, rather than to bypass it with an argument that eliminates it from the start. And since it is Deborah who holds office underneath the palm tree that bears her name, since it is toward her that the Israelites ascend for judgment, she, and not Barak, seems to me the right place to begin. Precisely what, then, is this activity of which she is the most exemplary representative?

In the narrative as in the song, Deborah is represented in the performance of a complex function. In the song, she is a poetess, in direct communication with the divine; poetry and prophecy are thus inseparable. She represents herself as responsible for the reversal of the catastrophe encompassing the land: precisely as "deliverer." Barak is hardly mentioned. She describes her own activity in a rather remarkable fashion: although the occasion is military, she describes no military *action* of which she is the stated subject. Instead, it is the stars who battle, and Yahweh the warrior who leads the combat. Lind (1980) finds this representation serene, pacific, which seems to me excessively idealistic, but the fact is, there is a substantial difference between the role of Deborah as she describes it and that, to give only one example, of Shamgar, a pureblood "liberator" if ever there was one: "And after him was Shamgar the son of Anath. He slew of the Philistines six hundred men with an ox goad and he too delivered Israel" (3:31). And this precursor of Samson is not alone in this book where slaughter abounds. How, then, can the poetess boast to have saved the land? It is clear that the claim has little substance except within a particular conception of cosmic organization, in which the unity between different domains prevails over separation. She has saved Israel by her faith, by her contact with Yawheh, with whom she is but one; by her clairvoyance, her poetry, by her good *judgment*. The

power of her song is testimony to this: there is nothing the right word*
cannot do. Thus she offers, for whoever knows how to listen, an explanation of what it means to *judge:* to pronounce the right word in a given
situation. It means, in other words, *to establish order in the chaos by means of
the right word.* Understood in this sense, the function reminds us of the
creation as it is represented in Genesis 1, which explains at the same time
why poetry, a verbal creative activity, forms an integral part of the function, and why this function is exercised in direct relation to the divine.
This view deepens that of Coogan (1978), who underlines on several
occasions the parallel between Deborah and Yahweh within the diegesis
of the song. For Coogan, it is the military performance that above all
establishes the parallel. The conception of *špt* I have just proposed explains why the parallel is possible in the first place.

In the narrative of chapter 4, the function is no longer represented in
exactly this way. Nevertheless, verse 4 allows of no misunderstanding:
Deborah was an autonomous judge, in office. An interesting philological
problem arises here. Many commentaries supply the complement traditionally rendered as "wife of Lappidoth" with a question mark. Long ago
Moore (1892) suspected that the "proper noun" was rather a modifier.
According to Boling (1975), the word can be an abstract form of the
common noun meaning /torch/. Woman of flames, of light? The epithet
would be highly appropriate. Deborah, enlightened judge, woman of
action, inspired and inspiring poetess, well deserves such a denomina-
tion. Moreover, the word, which is rare, is in the feminine inflection.
However plausible this interpretation may appear, all the translations I
consulted, including that of Boling, who cites the problem in a note,
retain "wife of Lappidoth." Boling interprets the noun as the surname of
the husband, none other than Barak, whose name means /lightning/. It
is not difficult to see how the concept of judge is altered by this husband
springing out of nowhere, which is to say, out of a dubious translation.
"Woman of" does not necessarily mean /spouse of/; the expression
means first of all, simply: /woman of/, /human being of feminine gender, qualified as/. The sequence /Deborah, a woman—prophetess, a
woman—of flames/ seems much more coherent—both semantically and,
by its parallelism, formally—than the one, based on a transformation of
the meaning of the word *'iššâ*, /Deborah, a woman prophetess, the wife
of Lappidoth/. As if to resolve this problem of semantic shift, the first
mention of *'iššâ* is omitted. Perhaps it is judged superfluous by the feminine ending of the word prophetess. Still the inflection is marked in the

*French has one word where English has two: *juste* can mean either "just" or "right," so
that *la juste parole* represents an extremely rich association of words: both the "right word"
in the poetic sense, as in *le mot juste*, and the "just word" of the legal sphere, the wisdom of
the judge.—TRANS.

Hebrew also, and the definite article is missing at both occurrences of
'*iššâ*.

To challenge Mr. Lappidoth's existence is not necessarily of great
consequence. Once the husband named Lappidoth is ruled out, the
proper noun alone, and not the interpretation of the common noun
as /spouse/ is questioned. If the husband exits from the scene, the institution of the husband is preserved. The position of judge would then be
shared by two people, a couple in the modern sense, with the woman
holding the office while the man leads the army. Indeed, in Heb. 11:32,
Barak is represented as the judge, and Deborah is no longer even mentioned. It is clear that the code, still on the basis of the separation of the
two aspects of the function of judge, serves an interest here; it supports
the division of labor according to the sexes, found, as the anthropology
books so often declare, "in all the cultures of the world" (Kloos 1981). If
Lappidoth the husband is absolutely superfluous, his exclusion is instrumental in the promotion of his "colleague." The assimilation of Lappidoth to Barak, who thereby becomes co-judge, constitutes a typical
case of the biased use of the code, assisted by the philological code,
which ultimately *permits* all three hypotheses.

The elimination of the prophetess is difficult to justify, of course,
considering the power Barak acknowledges she exerts—over him and
others. Boling (1975:109) cites Obermann, who emphasizes the combination of functions in other communities: "The pagan poet is not only
a spokesman but as a rule also a chieftain and warrior of his clan and
even of his tribe, so that he often describes raids he himself has insti-
gated, days in which he has taken a leading part." It is obviously crucial
for our understanding of the two versions to accept that, first, according
to the representation as it stands, Deborah could effectively have had
decisive power over the war, the soldiers, and their leader; second, that
she exercised her function normally, in all its complexity.

In the narrative, the function is not performed in the act of enunciation itself. It is described indirectly. This indirect perspective makes it
possible to show other aspects of the function, like the localization of the
office and the ascent of the people coming to appeal to her judgment. If
the poetic aspect is neglected, the prophetic aspect is enhanced in the
single exploit that is related: that of inspiring, *by the right word*, the instrument of the divine project to accept his role. Barak is neither hero, nor
deliverer, nor judge. He is nothing but the object of the mission, a victim
of dishonor, the executioner of what is already preordained, blind because without faith, and his association with Deborah's function is justified in no way whatsoever, except by modern readers' incomprehension
before the almost absolute power of the judge.

The question the anthropologist addresses to both texts—what is a
judge?—can find an answer only in the comparison of the two versions,

recognized as different yet dialectically related. The literary *genre*, implying a particular situation of enunciation, appears to be relevant and even descriptive of the distinct functions of the chapters. What the lyric song could not *say*, it *was:* word of the judge—the right word. That is how poetry is defined, even today. It was necessary that the detailed explanation precede its illustration; hence the priority of the narrative, in which poetry was redefined as prophetic word and in which the interlocutor was presented in order that the public understand the consequences of the right word—bringing about order—and of the failure to appreciate it—bringing about chaos. But language is a poor substitute for the event, and the explanation of the judge's word, preceding the poetry, obscured it.

The analysis of the concept of *špṭ* has shown the anthropological code at work in two directions. It imposed closure, clouded the eyes of critics obstinately projecting upon their object of study concepts taken to be universal—the separation of powers, for example—concepts whose application is historically limited. The critics in question did not abide by the first rule of anthropology: to regard the other not as an object but as the subject that speaks for itself. On the other hand, interpreting the concept of judge as I have just proposed permits us, once again, to differentiate in another way. Accepting the unity of the concept judge-liberator, to which we can add, in the "ideal" case of Deborah, poet-prophet, we see more clearly how the two versions differ. The difference will prove to be significant. To the extent that poetry's power in the present of the enunciation is replaced in the narrative by the prophetic link between past and future, the masculine figure will be able to take his place in the history of the imagination, of which our two chapters represent two phases. Thus, the concept of judge, which is a restrictive code if it is preinterpreted, can become a fertile code if we abstain from jumping to unambiguous conclusions. What we must do, then, is reestablish the whole network of meaning that the code directs, until it functions like the anthropological other, the respected and understood informant.

The Ethnographic Context

In the preceding section the anthropological code functioned to interpret the "public" side of the story. It will function now in the "private" domain, the assassination of Sisera. This part of the story presupposes a knowledge of tribal and nomadic life without which certain textual elements are meaningless. If we ignore the implications of the tribes' semi-nomadic life, verse 4:11, which clarifies the comings and goings of Jael's clan, will be difficult to understand. We must know that the task of pitching the tent was the women's responsibility if we are not to be surprised that Jael has the instruments of the murder at her disposal. At a level less emphatic but just as important, knowledge of the process of assimilation between the inhabitants of the land and the newcomers, a dynamic, continuous process that is never complete, constitutes the anthropological background that explains Sisera's error: the peace with Heber (or with the group this name can also designate) in no way guarantees the loyalty of the woman. The relative freedom a woman possessed in political and religious matters is thereby clarified as well.

It is not the referential and historical "truth" that is at stake when we speak of codes. As we have seen, such truth cannot be isolated from the imaginary representation whose object it is. Whether or not the Israelites of the epoch lived as nomads, the fact remains that the recognition of the content /life of nomads/, with all that it implies, is indispensable for understanding numerous elements in both texts. It is precisely for this reason that the anthropological code can mediate the conflict between the historical and the literary code. Anthropological reality *includes** in its interpretation the imaginary structure of the society, while the historical code attempts arbitrarily to exclude it.

This mediation can establish itself through the illuminating distinction that Geertz (1983) proposed between *experience-near* and *experience-distant* concepts. This distinction will prove capable of explaining *simultaneously* the content of the scene of the murder and the indignation it generally arouses. Let us take, as an example of an experience-near concept, the law of *hospitality;* the experience-distant concept, which corresponds to the first and embraces it, is that of *ritual* (Turner 1980). The first accounts for the "historical truth," that is, for the manner in which, according to tradition, the contemporaries represented, in their imagination, the "necessary" order of things; the second attempts simultaneously to describe, to interpret, and to explain the dynamics of this represented imagination. The scenes of the meeting of Jael and Sisera and of the death that ensues, gain in interest if one interprets them, according to the anthropological code, as highly ritualized. Attempts at an interpretation of ritual can be found in several commentaries, and they deserve to be integrated into a more general perspective.

First of all, we should note that the initiative is Jael's. It is she who offers hospitality to Sisera the fugitive. We know that hospitality toward strangers was, in the Mediterranean of antiquity, a fundamental rule. It was absolutely indispensable for the traveler's safety, which was always menaced, and therefore it was sacred (for the Greek example, see Finley 1977; Griffin 1980). In principal it was the traveler who asked for hospi-

---

*The French *comprendre* has two senses, so that the author is saying that anthropology attempts both to *understand* the imaginative domain of different societies and to *include* that domain within its own disciplinary boundaries.—TRANS.

tality; in the case where the host offered it, safety was guaranteed along with the invitation. The transgression of this rule was considered as the utmost act of treachery. So compulsory was this rule that its infraction came to resemble the transgression of a taboo.

To approach a stranger in an act of greeting, to address him saying, "turn in to me": the procedure is ritual. Dhorme (1956:730) compares it to Lot's invitation to the messengers of the Lord (given the outcome of this meeting, the reversed "rape" of Lot by his daughters, the comparison is interesting for still other reasons). Neil (1975:156), Cundall (1968:88, 100), and Dhorme (1956:730) mention the transgression of the rule of hospitality, and indignation is often heatedly expressed. This reaction must be because for them, the concept is experience-near and they do not take the necessary step in their analysis of applying the experience-distant concept. It is striking that the scene of the meeting, in which the number of reassuring expressions and actions is in fact quite elevated, is found only in the epic version. Next, the comparison with Gen. 19:3 has its pertinence, but so does that with a scene of false hospitality in the book of Judges itself, 19:20 and following. This parallel is passed over in silence by all the authors consulted, who, moreover, do not fail to invoke Judith and Delilah. We need only remember that in 19:20 the victim was a woman, victimized in atrocious fashion, to understand why this disturbing case is not evoked.

The concept of ritual allows other comparisons. If the words "turn in to me" constitute part of the ritual of hospitality, Jael pronounces others, equally ritual: "Fear not." If only the ritual of hospitality were concerned, these words would be superfluous. The invitation by itself dispels all grounds for fear. But these words are put into the mouth of Yahweh in Josh. 11:6, when he exhorts Joshua in the battle of Haron (against Jabin!). According to Deuteronomy (1:29; 7:18; 20:1), it is the ritual expression of encouragement in combat. Jael, in pronouncing it, sets a double and contradictory ritual in motion, and this double register, which the anthropological concept of ritual illuminates, will turn out to be central to the interpretation of the scene that follows. In offering Sisera more than he asks for, Jael in effect does battle with him. If Boling cites the second aspect, he draws no conclusions from it; the other commentators, ready to denounce Jael for the infraction of the rule of hospitality, do not even mention it. The anthropological code is stopped short halfway through its course, diverted toward the moral code, which sometimes glaringly takes the upper hand: "The seemingly generous action . . . , thus lulling him into a false sense of security, was the prelude to an act that, as has been noted, broke every accepted standard of hospitality" (Cundall 1968:100), or: "It is plain that she lured the fugitive to his doom and broke the sacred law of hospitality. . . . We cannot defend her. If we take the more lenient view, we can only say that she was another example of the patriotism which blinds the conscience" (Gillie and Reid 1924:216).

The episode of the invitation is missing from the song. This fact is often ignored. The identification of the two versions, which immediately follows the preceding passage, is remarkable: "Deborah's high praise of her is not to be taken as any proof of God's approval, but only as a sign of the imperfect moral life of the foremost believer of the day" (Gillie and Reid 1924:216). It seems to me that the differences, on this point, between the epic and the lyric versions signify the presence, in each of the respective versions, of opposing gender codes. The emphasis upon the initial meeting in the more recent, epic version will have to be explained; this emphasis alone justifies the judgment of Jael as a traitress.

Provided that it is applied where the theme is textually signified, the ritualistic anthropological code is very effective. If the meeting in chapter 4 is twice ritualized, the scene within the tent can also be interpreted by means of this code. There the theme of hospitality is further elaborated. First, when Sisera asks for water, Jael gives him milk. This time it is Sisera who takes the initiative, but Jael of her own will gives him more. Many interpreters see in this "seemingly generous action" (Cundall 1968:95) a second proof of treachery, because it reassures. The anthropological code can intervene here at several levels. At the referential level, it will furnish an indispensable item of information. The fact is that the milk here is curdled goat's milk, something always available in the tents of nomads. To substitute milk for the water requested thus represents in itself nothing extraordinary. Furthermore, this goat's milk has soporific qualities, which brings Boling to say: "She duped him and doped him" (98). This fact, unlike the other, contributes to the interpretation cited, adding fuel to the theme of /treachery/.

Once the concept of ritual is adopted, it shows itself operative at still another level. The anthropological code refers the interpretation to the ritual customs surrounding water, a vital element in the desert. To ask for water does not only belong to the ritual of hospitality; superimposed as a connotation, it also forms part of the ceremonial (s)election of wives. Let us see what happens, for example, when Abraham's servant goes in search of a wife for Isaac (Genesis 24), in the scene known as "the wooing of Rebekah." It was necessary that she be of the Hebrew people (24:3) and, moreover, that she be ready to follow the servant to the land of Abraham (24:8). Needless to say, beauty and virginity were equally requisite (24:16). Now, the fixed procedure, predetermined, for so demanding a selection, consists in asking a woman for water. *If she gives more*, she is the chosen. The procedure is recounted four times: fixed in advance (14), it is carried out (18, 19), and then related twice afterwards (43–44 and 45–46), a repetition that, in itself, already ritualizes. The interpreter who adopts the anthropological code at this ritualistic level will perhaps conclude that Jael is guilty of treachery, but hers would be a different kind of treachery: she behaves not only as a hostess but also as a ritually chosen sexual partner. Such an interpretation will be attentive to other actions that may have seemed of little or no significance, like the repeated act of "covering" before and after drinking. This act, some believe, is part of the ceremony preparatory to sexual intercourse (Prov. 7:16–18), while others (Zakovitch 1981:370–71) identify it as an insertion that censors, covering (!) the sexual scene by its connotation of innocence. Unfortunately, the name of the object doing the covering, *s'mika*, is unique, and no certitude whatsoever exists concerning its meaning. The sexual isotopy thus introduced is treated in two opposing manners. Either it is labeled as a motif, without being integrated into the total thematic network, or (Zakovitch 1981) it is elevated to the rank of unique theme, in a procedure I will discuss later as the use of the *thematic* code.

The scene is much briefer in the song, where the repetition in ascending progression (5:25), as characteristic of lyric poetics as it is of ritual, stresses the *honor* that is accorded Sisera. Since the isotopy of hospitality is now absent, so is the treachery. The contrast between the honorable reception—"a lordly bowl"—and the dishonorable death—"the workmen's hammer"—would seem, at first glance, to stress the theme recurrent throughout the book: the *shame* that falls on the masculine figure to be killed by a woman. The book of Judges alone offers three examples, and in the texts just as much as in the commentaries this shame is thematized. In the absence of the isotopy of betrayed hospitality, which leads quickly to Jael's condemnation, that of shame, even while implying a negative evaluation of women, devalues first of all the victim. Curiously, the song, which enhances the second motif, does not otherwise make it explicit; the narrative, which offsets that motif with the alternate isotopy of treachery, cites it even while *doubling* it: Barak is punished for his cowardice in soliciting the protection of Deborah on the battlefield, but his punishment is the shame of seeing his enemy killed by a woman—the shame of the other's shame. Once the anthropological code has put us on the track of this theme, it will become interesting to follow its evolution through chapter 4, where it is both more persistent and more problematic, entangled as it is in the compensatory network of treachery.

Understood in this way, the anthropological code can provide much more than referential information. It illuminates thematic elements that structure the text, and thus makes it possible to glimpse profound differences between the two versions; differences that, without its help, would go unperceived.

A final example illustrates this code's capacity to protect the hermeneutic enterprise from the consequences of ethnocentrism and its sexist variant. In the song of Deborah, there is a final stanza that has no equivalent in the narrative. It is the stanza on Sisera's mother, who anxiously awaits the return of her son.

> At the window she looked out and cried,
> through the lattice, the mother of Sisera,
> why is his chariot so slow to come
> why do the hoofbeats of his chariot delay?

> The wisest of her princesses answered,
> nay, to herself she answered:

> Are they not finding and dividing the spoil,
> one womb/girl, two wombs/girls for each hero's head,
> spoil of dyed cloth for Sisera,
> spoil of dyed cloth embroidered,
> dyed cloth twice embroidered for his neck?

The attention to maternal sentiments is often regarded as the indication of a feminine gender code, an anachronistic interpretation to which I will return. What I want to consider here is the little motif of the embroidered scarf that appears at the very end. The stanza is rich in anthropologically interesting motifs: the women imprisoned in their passivity behind the windows, as behind the lattice that one still sees today in oriental architecture (Van Dijk-Hemmes 1983); the entourage of women, doubtless those of the nobility of the court, who vie in wisdom with Deborah, the true sage; and, especially, the motif that has attracted the most attention: the "wombs," the prisoners, distributed to "each hero's head." Of the four verses devoted to the description of the spoil falsely presupposed, only one deals with the prisoners, and three with the embroidered scarf, in ascending progression: the dyed cloth, the embroidered dyed cloth, the twice-embroidered dyed cloth—for his neck. Clearly the colors and the embroidery are significant—but of what?

Dhorme (1956:73) is quick to find the solution: "Ce sont des femmes qui parlent, d'où l'insistance sur les étoffes coloriées et brodées" (These are women speaking, hence the insistence upon colored and embroidered fabrics). Trapped by his own anachronistic perspective and diverted by the expression "parler chiffons" ("to talk fashion," which means "to talk about nothing, as women do"), common in modern French, the critic betrays a condescending attitude that predominates over the historical and anthropological perspective he otherwise adopts. We see how the ethnocentric code enforces closure. It is, in fact, a double-edged sword: not only does the critic project his own modern prejudices on another culture; what is more, in perpetuating the image of women preoccupied with frivolities, he confirms and fortifies that image—itself another prejudice. For if, in the eyes of this critic, the insistence is thus explained, the location of these verses at the end of the poem deflates the suspense that had been so skillfully created and devalues the text. The stanza ending with the trivialities of women can only be the doing of a clumsy poetess. Several aspects are thus lost sight of. The ironic opposition between two forms of wisdom, the false and the true (Van Dijk-Hemmes 1983), is ignored. Forgotten, next, is the surprise that awaits the mother, of which the listeners of the poem are already informed. What we have here is a specific type of suspense, the *inclusive secret:* the public shares it with the speaker, while the character is excluded from this collusion (see Bal 1985). The device is even richer than it appears at first glance. The mother asks a question, but the response of "the wisest of her princesses" is her own. The comparison with Deborah only becomes all the more poignant. In the Canaanite mother there is, without her knowing it, the shadow of a prophetic gift, as seen in the allusion to her son's death in the word translated as "neck." A synonym of the word translated as "temple" in the murder scene, it also means the tender part of the head. Her position of princess, however, noble but imprisoned, confers upon her no prophetic force except that corrupted by the alienation that makes her speak of other women as "wombs" to divide among the men, the thieves (violators)* of women (Van Dijk-Hemmes 1983). This is why she herself does not understand her own prophecy. The contrast between the two "mothers" has nothing to do with the sugar-sweet idea of maternity so predominant in our culture.

But all this does not yet explain the recurrence of the embroidered cloth. The anthropological code will be alert to the social value of the item. It was a precious commodity in the ancient Mediterranean world. A veritable *object of value* (Greimas and Courtès 1979:259) around which many an intrigue is built (Genesis 37), it makes its appearance here as the most valorized element of the spoil. Indeed, the interpreter using the anthropological code will refer the reader to Genesis 37, where the embroidered cloth of many colors given to Joseph as the sign of paternal election will later be the sign—again false—of his death, because its positive signification had been intolerable in the eyes of his nonelected brothers. In this way the song's conclusion becomes meaningful. A contrast is established between the embroidered piece, which should be the sign of a glorious life, and the rending of garments replaced by the ashen sackcloth, unembroidered, uncolored, sign of mourning. Jacob wears the sackcloth, but as Joseph is not dead, he does so mistakenly. Here the situation is reversed: the mother rejoices too soon, mistakenly, in the colored cloth. Explicit there, implicit here, the contrast between the two cloths consitutes the climax of the poem. The enemy is destroyed, but there is even more reason to rejoice for the victor; the news of his death will break the morale of his people for good. After the expectation of the embroi-

*Between the *thief,* "voleur," and the *violator,* "violeur" of women, the spoils of war, there is the difference of an "i."—TRANS.

dered scarf, the ashen sackcloth, not yet present but imminent, will weigh more heavily, paralyzing the enemy and consecrating the victory.

Understood in this fashion, the anthropological code sheds light on features otherwise incomprehensible and therefore quickly condemned. It contributes to the understanding not only of the meaning of these features but of their function throughout the text, indeed throughout the culture of the time. It opens the interpretation to different cultural properties and thus guards against the errors caused by the "effect of strangeness" that Eco describes (1976:18) implicitly in the passage ana- lyzed above. Geertz's conceptual scheme, characteristic of alert and well- informed anthropological discourse, makes it possible to establish the crucial connection between the "historical reality" with which we began our examination of codes and the imaginary representation where it comes to rest. This important connection is founded on the "transla- tion," of which only anthropology is capable, of experience-near con- cepts into experience-distant concepts. Belonging to the second cate- gory, the concept of ritual is relevant here, but to demonstrate that there are other possible concepts, that of object of value was also cited. An- thropology, in turn, functions thanks to the contribution of the two disciplines between which it plays a mediating role: any separation be- tween historical reality and the imagination would deprive anthropology of its very foundation.

The Oral Code

A third series of observations on the anthropological code concerns an aspect still closer to literary preoccupations: the relationship of both versions to some background of orality. In a sense, this is the most important aspect, because it challenges the existence, the very possibility of the texts. Today, specialists agree in acknowledging an oral back- ground to the texts of the Hebrew Bible that must have profoundly influenced the form in which they were preserved. The original oral background of these texts is difficult for our minds to conceive, ac- customed as we are to centuries of the written transmission of texts. One consequence of such a background is that the question of the authenticity or originality of the text loses all significance. There is no original; there were only different oral traditions in which these stories or poems or fragments were recounted or sung. In this sense, it is not even certain that the lyric version of chapter 5 was available as a source to the narrator of chapter 4. The most one can say is that the redactors who put together the twenty-one chapters of the book, probably in the time of the monarchy, had both versions at their disposal; the examination can only begin there.

Probably there were other versions that were not inserted. We do not know exactly; but we do know that, for one reason or another, the decision was made to put the more recent version before the older. This is an extraordinary decision. Even if any explanation can be hypothetical at best, the argument most often proposed is weak. The redactors, it goes, would have first given the more "factual" version, which relates what happened, and then followed it with the poetic celebration. We have already seen, and will see again in even greater detail, to what extent such a view depends upon a particular conception of the "factual," of the historical. The circularity of the argument makes us forget that the choice made was not the only possible one; for example, the two versions could have been integrated to form an ensemble. Deborah the singer could have been cited, so that the song would logically follow or precede, or be embedded in, the narrative. The very separation of the versions is perhaps as significant as their order. I will later defend the hypothesis that the priority of the narrative is the priority of the male perspective characteristic of a certain culture: modern, educated, and historiographical. The narrative includes elements missing from the song, and putting the more recent text before the older one obscures, no doubt, precisely what was not "factual" but superimposed, for specific reasons that remain to be clarified.

In what sense can we speak of an orality of the texts? The theoretical knowledge we possess of how the texts functioned within a system of orality operates as a code when we interpret certain characteristics—stylistic or other—of the texts by its light. Sometimes it becomes instrumental in explaining problematic elements, like repetitions. The code thus helps us escape from logocentric ethnocentrism, which claims that all repetition is a waste of energy. Sometimes, on the other hand, the code is used, paradoxically, to stop the process of interpretation, to minimize the differences between the two versions by relegating them to the "primitive" or "ornamental" oral system. The terms orality and poetry are interchangeable in this type of discourse. Witness the following example (Cundall 1968:100): "The repetitions in the poetical account, together with the uncertainty in translating several of the verbs in this description, account for most of the differences between this and the prose account." This type of discourse is characterized by the vague use of the terms "orality" and "poetry." This is a negative use of the code: the hermeneutic question—what do the differences signify?—receives the answer: they signify orality, that is, uncertainty and futility.

Even while remaining a factor of uncertainty (but what isn't in this domain?), the code can be a much more effective instrument in the hands of other researchers. There it takes on a meaning that, implicitly or explicitly, recognizes in the concept of orality the sign of differentiation from our own literate culture. There are far-reaching consequences in such an attitude. Zumthor (1984:67) makes it very clear that we are concerned here not with a certainty that is accessible or even desirable, but with an epistemological starting point that seeks an alternative to the rigid and reductive presuppositions inherent in the literate system. What Zumthor proposes as the goal of a "hermeneutics of orality" is exactly what we need here: "What I am seeking to evoke in this way would be a 'poetic' discourse, homogeneous with its subject matter, as opposed to an approved master language that is external and reductionist: a language that is both everchanging and yet producing its adherence to truth: a gesture" (73).

It is in this spirit that I have tried to approach the concept of *judge*. It will *a fortiori* have to govern all our research in the domain of orality. Note at the start the particular sense the code of orality assumes here. Its goal is not to establish the exact limits between oral sources and ancient poetry. This code, like every other code, dictates an *attitude*, one that, in the present case, acknowledges the uncertainty, the variation, and the central place of the situation of enunciation. It opens the mind of the interpreter to a "forgotten" functioning of language. Ong (1984:6), opposing it to learned Latin, describes it thus: "Learned Latin left all its users free of the rich, emotional, unconscious, but often confusingly subjective involvements of a language learned orally from infancy, where knower and known, subject and object, formed a kind of continuum that could be broken up only gradually and perhaps never completely." These implications are harrowing; Suleiman (1987) employs, in a completely different context, the eloquent term *entanglement* in order to analyze their effects upon rational man confronted with what he does not understand. To follow the code of orality is to acknowledge the traces of these implications; it becomes much more than a mere technical code.

To what extent can features of orality be discerned? Blenkinsopp (1961:64) attributes the following characteristics to the orality of the poem:

> The frequent dramatic juxtapositions, so effective for holding attention and directing it to the essentials in the story, the vivid dialogue with dramatic repetitions, the use of poetical words and the constant hammering on proper names, the names of dramatis personae, the catch phrases, puns, and strong sonic patterns, all calculated to spin out the story and hold the attention of the hearer to what is being told—the age-old art of the story teller, in short.

Among the formal characteristics enumerated here, most figure in the long list established by Walter Ong (1982:31–77). It would still be necessary to add what is perhaps the best-known characteristic: the formulae (Lord 1960), standard expressions that, even more than the words of the language, were supposed to be the stock material available to the oral poet. As Bäuml (1984) suggested, Lord's theory needs to be elaborated. If we were to apply it as it stands, we could suppose that not only the repeated expression "blessed be Yahweh," but also turns of phrases like "in the days of . . ." (5:6), structures like "from heaven they fought . . ." (5:20), that is, complements of place + verb + subject, belong to the category of such formulae. (Cp. "At the window she looked out and cried, through the lattice, the mother of Sisera," 28; "For the divisions of Reuben there were great thoughts of heart," 15.) Globe (1978:162–65) considers still many other elements formulaic. A comparison with Psalm 68 shows that the author of the latter was probably inspired by the song of Deborah. The list of tribes is also treated as formulaic. Given the importance accorded this list by the historians, the argument of orality is worth hearing:

> Such lists have in common a tendency to "include more information than is required" for the story; this suggests an independent existence for most of them outside of their final contexts. But they were incorporated by poets into their poems "even at some loss to the narrative" probably because their audience expected them. (Globe 1978:163)

The reason for this expectation could not be elaborated in the limited space of Globe's article. I think we will find an answer in the cognitive function of poems belonging to the oral system. Here, this function is again very skillfully integrated: in what is a nationalistic poem, we learn what constitutes this nation we are called upon to support. The cognitive function thus becomes twice as effective in integrating itself with the function of persuasion. The argument is interesting to the extent that it integrates, like other notions that we have seen, the "historical truth" and the representation of what we imagined this truth to be. The theory of formulae warrants further consideration, however.

It leads, for Lord, to the description of characteristic features of oral composition; it justifies those features which might seem merely inept to the ear of the literate listener. The orality of the compositions he studied, heard on location, is incontestable. To invert the theory, however, and expect it to lead us back to the oral background of a written text, is a very different matter. The oral code cannot be used in this way. Bäuml (1984), in a convincing plea for the refinement of the theory, distinguishes several phases or types of orality. Even when orality is certain, the situation of oral composition does not necessarily correspond to a situation of oral performance: a minstrel is not always a poet. *A fortiori,* we must distinguish between primary orality and the presence of formulae and other indices of orality in a text that we know only in its written form. For the text as we have it is in fact a written text composed in relation to an oral tradition. It is thus necessarily, among other things, a commentary on its own source. This commentary may represent a positive or negative attitude toward orality. Furthermore, such a text *fictionalizes* the oral situation, which thereby becomes a "character" in the written text, a character that we recognize through certain basic attributes. Of these, *authority* is the most characteristic. In the oral tradition, the poet is the one who *knows;* the cognitive function of the poetry is clearly marked.

In light of what we have just learned, certain questions lose their significance. Whether the song of Deborah is a primary oral source, and Deborah its author, or a literary text of only secondary, fictive orality, in which Deborah procures her authority from another narrator, has little relevance for the discussion of codes. In both cases, orality, fictive or not, assigns authority to the poetess, fictive or not, as source of the events recounted, fictive or not, which are focalized by Deborah. The enthusiasm the event calls forth is considered the source of the inspiration of her song, her *šîr;* her *act,* represented as oral, of singing, sets up the representation of a dialectical relation between the event and its celebration. Within the whole, the subjects of the enunciation of the focalization and of the action are inseparable; they coincide. It is this fusion of the act and the result of representation that is exemplified by the oral situation. To conserve the traces of that situation in a written text is a positive act of commentary; this is how the song becomes meaningful. We have seen to what degree the function of *judge* has to be tied to the word. It is in the song, which offers the representation of that connection, and only there, that we can catch a glimpse of what the use of the word, that is, orality, meant in Hebraic antiquity—not as the technical basis of the transmission of texts, but as a principle of communication. When certain aspects of the text are interpreted in this way, there is no reason whatsoever to close the interpretation. The poetess must have used the structures of orality—traditional or truly mnemonotechnical structures, it hardly matters—while pursuing a more specific goal. This explains how she could construct series of ascending progressions in which repetition is enrolled in the service of the emotion or of the emphasis that guides the interpretation.

The frequency of proper nouns, considered by Blenkinsopp to be a characteristic of orality, constitutes an interesting case. Indeed, if we start with the premise of orality, then we must also posit a situation of performance, parallel to the *Sitz-im-Leben* invoked by Lapointe (1977). The text verbalizes a specific situation that individualizes it. Any written version of an oral performance loses the contact with the different levels of enunciation that is inherent in orality. In our case, what we risk losing without the help of the oral code is precisely the act by which the singer attracted, as she named them, the members of the tribe both to the song—in the present—and to the war—in the past. The "right word" also means the well-placed appeal to the addressee, recognized and specified by the most significant of proper names, that of the tribe, which mutually relates all its members. Zumthor's expression (1984:83) receives here an exemplary richness: the word institutes a dialogue with its own theme.

Comparing both versions from the perspective of orality, we immediately realize that an examination of this kind is impossible without accounting for certain truly literary aspects, notably, the difference of genres. This is why we will return to the subject later. The fact remains that, beyond these generic differences, the song, contrary to the narrative, thematizes the situation of orality and meets, in other respects as well, the criteria developed by Ong independently from this case.

We must suppose that the narrative, forming more directly a sequence with the other chapters of the book, was reworked more freely than the song; the latter, only slightly modified ("showing few traces of early or late liturgical adaptation," Boling 1975:117), was transcribed in the form in which it circulated. In other words, by dint of being sung and being popular, it became relatively untouchable: relatively because the situation of orality excluded the possibility of repetition verbatim; untouchable because it was already so integrated as common cultural property that it could not be reworked from top to bottom to satisfy ideological or theological ends. This inviolability explains the attempts of a number of theologians to modify, or at least to criticize, the poem's theology. The same cannot be said for the narrative, even if it too has an oral background. Belonging to the epic (oral) tradition, it could more easily be integrated within the project and unified writing of this tradition.

This being the case, it is hardly astonishing that elements were *added* in the more recent version, although it is still necessary to interpret the motivation behind the supplements. But that one removed certain elements, under these conditions, is remarkable, and the first task of the code of orality will be to seek out the motivations that governed these suppressions, which appear to be acts of censorship. The censorship in question first suppresses traces of orality: neither the thematization of the oral situation nor the other "oral" features of the song find their way into the narrative. We can suppose that a specific interest could have ordered this suppression. Indeed, the ideological importance of the transition from orality to writing is something that no longer needs to be demonstrated (Havelock 1963). More recently, Lemaire (1984) insisted on the intimate relationship between the development of the written system, the formation of nations, and the centralization of power that ensued. This suggests a domination of the masses by an elite as much as an evolution toward a narrow rationalism. The integration of these aspects takes shape in the project of a "national" historiography based on conquest, centralization, and the predominance of the male line. Here we have, I believe, important evidence for the priority of chapter 4. Its orality must have been more firmly suppressed because this text was made to fit into the new historiographic tradition. Such suppression was possible because the oral background of the text was part of what preceded and prepared this tradition: the epic tradition. The commentators who propose the argument of the greater "factuality" of the epic version adopt the same code of literacy that must have dictated the order of the two chapters; it attempts to relegate the lyric version, of a more thematized and therefore durable oral base, to a secondary, ornamental function, which means it comes "after" the writing of history.

The seductive power of this project—and of the interest that lies behind it—is all the more obvious since a number of excellent critics make themselves its ready accomplice without their knowing it. One of these is Kugel, who writes his fascinating study like a crusade against anachronistic interpretation, and who does not tire of denouncing the presuppositions of the exegetical tradition. But he falls victim to the very illusion that he brings to light at precisely this point. Speedily discounting the arguments in favor of an old poetic oral background, which would have dictated the priority of the song, he suggests that writing, at the time of composition, was still rare, the privilege of the elite, and thus he does not see what possible interest could have been served in forcing the transition to writing at the expense of orality. The naïveté in a critic so intelligent is striking. First of all, the fact that the transition did take place is undeniable; it follows that there must have been an interest that determined it, that profited by it. Second, the very elitism of writing was at stake in the battle against orality. There lies the interest of the elite in eliminating the oral traditions: more "democratic" because scattered and uncontrollable, they hampered the imposition of new relations of power.

In this light, the differences between the two versions can be explained even without (false) certainty regarding the textually rich oral base. It hardly seems plausible that, as early as the time of the editorial adaptation of chapter 4, the audience no longer understood the irony of the embroidered cloth presaging the ashen sackcloth, or the significance of the mourning paralyzing the enemy. The suppression of the final stanza cannot be the effect of incomprehension or a lapse of memory, so easily alleged in cases like this. Starting from the hypothesis that the song circulated and was an integral part of the oral tradition of the period in which the narrative was drafted, we will instead have to search for an explanation of the changes in the dual thematics of the narrative, in which the shame of Sisera is paralleled with the shame of Barak, and in which the coming and going in the tent of Jael is organized around deceived hospitality. Thus, the thematic and stylistic difference between the two versions deepens. New light is shed upon it by the code of orality, not only because there are different phases of orality, but also and especially because the "material," the act of Jael, was usurped by a project in which it could only be condemned and circumscribed by "rational" explanation—its meaning, its purpose, and its performance being neither acknowledgeable nor acceptable. We shall see later that this project of rational and nationalistic historiography implies the urgent need to justify, through an extremely circumspect and detailed narrative, Sisera's "stupidity" in having been "had."

The anthropological codes have important advantages over the codes already treated. This superiority is based on two features inherent in the anthropological enterprise itself. First, unlike the historical code, the anthropological codes are capable of interpreting the texts in their different textual aspects. In other words, they take account of the place and the function of the texts in a specific society. Without losing sight of the material and concretely historical foundations upon which the texts were able to come into being, they treat them as *representations*. By this means they are capable of integrating two often incompatible perspectives, and thus they undermine the binary and aporistic opposition between reality and fiction. Not that the anthropological codes by definition protect the researcher from closure, anachronism, ethnocentrism, and androcentrism. We have seen some rather distressing evidence to the contrary. But the fact remains that the anthropological project stimulates a critical attitude toward these biases. Second, contrary to the theological code too easily superimposed on the religious code, the anthropological codes underline, on the one hand, the differences between the ways of life in force in the culture of the texts and in our own, and on the other, the significance of acts that, gratuitous to our eyes, are ritualistic in context. The result is that these codes are capable of contributing to the critical enterprise by actively resisting the anachronistic prejudices that pass unnoticed with the help of the ethnocentric code. Paradoxically, it is through the acceptance of the imagination that the anthropological codes succeed in opening the mind to a reality different from, but as real as, our own.

·4·

THE LITERARY CODE

The interpretive methods commonly used by literary interpreters most often consist of combinations of codes of diverse origin: psychoanalysis, linguistics, logic, etc. The present chapter will not concern this group of codes. A certain discourse, recognizable as *literary* discourse, is distinguished by the use of words like *genre, structure, metaphor, irony, emphasis, repetition,* as well as by judgments of aesthetic value. It is the discourse we employ when we seek to characterize a text as literary, to reveal its composition, or to detect the sources of the beauty we see in it. This discourse is based upon a code that is as plural as the anthropological code, and that is recognizable by a concern for order and an avidity for meaning, whose necessary plurality is willingly conceded. The code that directs this discourse is based first of all upon a suspension of correspondence to reality. It is situated at the other end of the scale of disciplines treated here, diametrically opposed to historical research. Literary studies have never succeeded in resolving the problem of the relation to reality, in spite of the exhaustive attempts of the sociocritics. It seems to me that this impasse is due to their decision to attempt an integration with history and sociology rather than with anthropology. The latter would have provided more appropriate concepts for bridging the gap between reality and imagination by analyzing the intimate dialectical relation between the two. This attitude of literary studies toward reality attains its culminating point in the autonomistic movements of the fifties and the sixties; it is recognizable in a tacit and almost inevitable declaration of ethical indifference. Neil (1975:157), speaking of Judges 5, expresses this last feature as in passing, hence, as something too obvious to dwell on: "If the morality is questionable the poetry is superb." This indifference, which goes so far as a hostility toward all social criticism, considered a form of censorship, was broken more or less effectively by feminist criticism. True, there were other attempts, but the feminist critics adopted a different attitude. They sought less to resolve the problem in theory than to reject it in practice. Trible (1976, 1984) is the best-known example in the field of biblical exegesis. Ethical indifference, and the opposition between ethics and aesthetics that it implies, as useful as it may have seemed for the freedom of the artist, has long paralyzed the literary critic, and modern literary exegesis shows the effects. I will try to demonstrate that this "indifference" in fact passionately masks specific interests.

It is in view of this discussion that I have refused to adopt a term that might seem more appropriate for the code at stake. Indeed, if the term *formalism* were not so tied to specific schools, the term *formal code* would almost impose itself. I prefer the term *literary code* for four reasons. First, the literary code, just as much as the theological code, is victim of the confusion between the meta-code of the critic and the personal literary code biased by her/his taste—necessarily anachronistic relative to the text. Second, if the literary code is inclined to gravitate toward form, this is in fact a polemic choice that is not inevitable and that, linked as it is to the separation between aesthetics and ethics, is questionable. Next, the domain in which the literary code functions is generally subdivided into *genres,* each of which, in turn, extends beyond the purely literary aesthetic domain. Whenever an element is interpreted within the framework of an ideal narrative structure, something we have already seen, the code applied is narratological and belongs, in this sense, to the literary code; it is at the same time aesthetic, and the second aspect is parasitic on the first, which serves as its alibi. Given the generic difference between our two versions, the analysis of interpretive acts based on the literary code, as acts based on several codes, subcodes, or superimposed codes, seems valuable. Finally, the way form is offered as an interpretive argument, through its relation to the content, which the critic assigns, a content that is necessarily implied in every process of interpretation, constitutes a problem that the very term *formalism* presupposes resolved.

The aesthetic or generic literary perspective functions as a code when the characteristic features of the text that are explicitly or implicitly attributed to its literariness direct the interpretation toward a thematic network that would otherwise be difficult to develop. This is what happens when the differences between the two versions are explained according to the genre adopted—for instance, attributing the expression of feeling to the lyric convention. This conception leaves diegetical chronology and even narrative suspense out of the picture. This is also what happens when, given the dual thematics already supposed in the narrative, we favor the line of shame because it makes it possible to see the death of Sisera ironically reflected in the failure of Barak. The play of speech acts versus physical acts (in the Hebrew Bible, mental acts are practically absent; see Alter 1981) in the scene of the murder is characteristic of the prose version. Guided by the literary code that illuminates the structure of this sequence of acts, we see that it signifies a power play in which the positions of the protagonists are twice reversed.

In the following pages, I will first analyze how the literary code, or the lyric subcode, uses aesthetics as an argument for assailing other codes, notably the historical code. We will see it work in its restrictive mode, imposing closure, rejecting certain possibilities as invalid. I will then show how, from the same perspective, the lyric subcode functions to oppose a possible gender code. The narratological subcode may carry out the same functions: rather than preparing the way for differentiated thematic interpretations, in practice it too often serves only to neutralize other codes under the pretext of aestheticism. The nongeneric literary code, characterized by a more diffuse aestheticism, is less strictly biased, and thus a more powerful instrument: it allows us to progress still further, and to intepret, not to condemn, certain textual features as lying at the source of specific codes, thus inverting the critical perspective.

The Polemic Lyric Code

One example of the lyric code as an instrument of censorship was already touched upon in the first chapter. Cundall (1968:92), who characterized the differences between the two versions as "slight dissimilarities," no doubt from the blinding perspective of the historical code, in the same passage declared lyric language to be "not always precise." We are left to assume that prose, on the other hand, is the language of precision. He spoke of "elaborations" and of "hyperboles" that would, in the song, be employed "to augment the effect." Still later, we saw, he attributed the differences to poetic repetitions. This example is representative of a great number of published critical works. The literary code, here, operates in the context of a polemic between two discourses. The underlying conception of this polemic can be represented as in fig. 4.

What we see emerging here is a conception not only of literature but of other discourses as well, in which History occupies the place of honor in the shadow of Truth, and which, even worse, allows this critic, like many others, to praise the aesthetic qualities of the song while at the same time condemning its insufficiency as a source—despite the superiority conceded to it in other respects. In belittling the documentary value of a text he appreciates as a masterpiece of poetry, the critic does away with the differences between the two versions. Imputable to the lyric form, these elements are *in excess.* Thus Cundall the historian, preoccupied with the background of the text, the content, ends up using the literary code precisely to dispose of that content. This is a paradoxical kind of formalism, where a code serves to make decoding superfluous. It leads inevitably to the separation of aesthetics and ethics, which alone can make the text a thing of pleasure for the moralizing critic. This pleasure is a liberation for whoever has endorsed the restriction of the narrow rationalism of the historiographic project; it responds to a vital need too

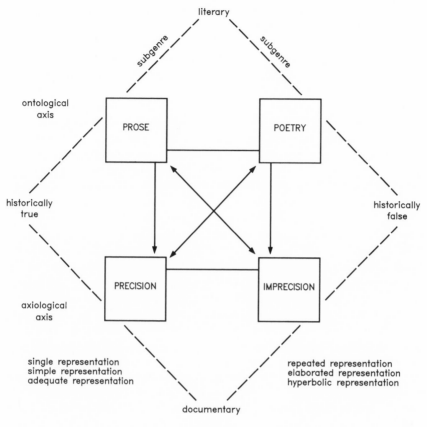

literary

subgenre

subgenre

ontological
axis

PROSE

POETRY

historically
true

historically
false

PRECISION

IMPRECISION

axiological
axis

single representation
simple representation
adequate representation

repeated representation
elaborated representation
hyperbolic representation

documentary

Fig. 4

often repressed. This need, in fact, can be satisfied only when all responsibility is eliminated. The separation of ethics and aesthetics is de-
manded with all the passion implied by this restriction.

Given the importance and the frequent appearance of the mechanism
at stake, I will analyze a few examples. Richter (1963), whom we have
already seen passionately defending certain preestablished distinctions,
justifies his approach within the literary code, whose basic premises remain implicit. His programmatic study *Exegese als Literaturwissenschaft*
(1971) formulates the theses upon which his previous studies were already based. His preference for form presupposes that it can be distinguished from content, that certainty regarding content can in the final
analysis be reached, and that literary genres, distinguished on the basis
of formal criteria, determine the content. The polemic stance this formu-
lation implies becomes obvious when the author makes a statement on
the value of the song:

> Schon die Gattung 'Poesie' muss davor warnen, diesen Abschnitt als
> historische Forsetzung des vorgehenden zu betrachten; den um histo-
> rische Dinge geht es in anderen Gattungen, zuvor der Prosa. (1963:94)

> Already the genre of "poetry" should warn us against regarding this
> fragment as historical documentation of what happened; it is in other
> genres, like prose, that we find historical things.

Here, the very presupposition of generic distinctions is in itself sufficient
to eliminate the text's content. Richter fully participates here in the
ideologeme of fig. 4. Kugel wrote his study (1981) precisely in opposition
to this kind of projection of the modern dichotomy. For Richter this
dichotomy is so obvious that he does not even bother to justify it. Later
(1971:155) he elaborates a much more detailed generic system, in which
ethical, narrative, and juridical genres are subdivided into several subgenres. Curiously, Richter does not return, in this theory of genres, to
the prose-poetry dichotomy that had been of such consequence in the
earlier study.

In a more recent and often cited article, Freedman (1977) shows how
important the prose-poetry dichotomy underlying the lyric code is. In a
positivist effort characteristic of a whole recent trend of literary studies,
the author defends the mechanical criterion of the presence or absence
of certain stylistic details. A computer-based analysis, we are told, has
proven that the particle *'et,* introductory sign of the direct object, the
relative pronoun *'ašer,* and the definite article *ha-,* frequent in prose, are
rare or absent in poetry. The analysis seems to have been executed with
precision, and the conclusions are cautiously drawn. Two elements crucial to all research of this genre are, however, lacking. First, the distinction made *a priori* is never justified. The conclusion that the absence of
indices proves that one is dealing with a poetic text is merely a restatement of the starting point. Next, the results are not analyzed. What does
the presence of these indices in fact mean? Given their syntactical functions, it is clear that they are, in fact, the symptoms of literate rationalism,
contrary to the more flexible oral discourse, which is based on juxtaposition. The particle *'et* reinforces the syntactical link between two elements,
eliminating ambiguity. The relative pronoun introduces the subordinate
clause, which replaces juxtaposition. The definite article, index of certitude and individuality, is emblematic of the whole historiographical project. Together the three indices refer to narration, the affirmative mode
in which the direct object, *the absent other* of whom one speaks, whose
history is fixed, eclipses the addressee, *the present other* with whom the lyric
poet speaks. It is less a question of genres than of linguistic attitudes.

Blind to the meaning of his own results, Freedman fails to justify the
connection between the statistical analysis and his interpretation of poetry as prophecy, elaborated in the second part of his article. This pro-

phetic function, inherent in poetry and socially vital, determines, as we have seen, the function of *judge*. Linked, as Freedman also points out, to inspiration, which gives it the authority characteristic of a judge, the prophetic function is thus usurped and replaced by historiography.

Considered in this way, the poetry of Deborah is thus neither one genre among others nor a pole of the prose-poetry dichotomy; both conceptions would presuppose contemporaneity and free choice. Rather it is the record of a linguistic and social attitude that was fought and then repressed. Freedman's analysis, which includes some highly valuable elements, traps the concept of poetry between two lyric codes, each unable to enrich the other: the mechanical code of unexplained syntax and the lyric code of romantic origin, which excludes true linguistic research.

The antihistorical lyric code is perhaps nowhere more explicitly tied to the interests of historiography than in Gerleman's study (1951), which claims to be stylistic. Enthusiasm for the literary beauty of what he calls "impressionistic description" betrays all the more clearly what is really at stake in the author's efforts. The differences between the two versions are not comparatively analyzed; as a believer in normative stylistics, the author lays down a norm from which the song represents a deviation. Speaking of the song's composition, Gerleman himself adopts the lyrical style in declaring, "The events have been strung together like pearls on a necklace, with no regard for their logical causes and consequences" (1951:171). "Lack of logic" will become the persistent theme of his analysis. Defending the unity of the poem, he sees it "more in the emotional ambience than in the composition, more in the emotional color than in the structure." What he had only a moment before called a technique, devoid though it was of logic, now becomes an absence of composition.

The negative constructions and the recurrence of words like "logic," "coherence," and "causality" in the critic's discourse illustrate all too clearly to what degree the anachronistic lyric code, the suppression of orality, and the project of historiography go hand in hand. The normative character of the analysis occasionally bursts forth in passages like this one:

> What should, according to a *logical analysis*, be depressed to the level of a subordinate or accessory conception will often become a dominant motif when seen by an impressionistic narrator, and what according to *all the claims of logic and consistency* should be *absolute essentials*, will be neglected. (172; my italics)

It should hardly surprise us that an author so sure of knowing, in the name of logic, what is essential and what is not, submits as his first example the "description of the battle" and condemns the almost complete absence of such description in a poem supposed to be the celebration of that battle. Among the details that "are missing" in this "descrip-

tion" are the Israelite army, the actions of the Canaanite kings, and an
elaborated portrayal of Sisera. "The *name* of the captain is mentioned
only incidentally, and the *preliminaries of the murder* are sketched in extremely cursorily" (172; my italics). The norm is represented by the more
recent version. This suggests a curious kind of methodology. And the
"facts" supposedly lacking are those that emphasize rather specific preoccupations: political history on the one hand, and explanation, the
excuse for Sisera's stupidity, on the other. "Logic" and "coherence" are
thus simply names for the ideology inherent in rationalist historiography, an ideology adopted, but never openly, by this critic preoccupied
with innocent-looking stylistics.

The Nonpolemic Lyric Code

It is possible to manipulate the lyric code without dividing it along the
line that separates poetry from prose. We then find ourselves in a position to address two aspects of the song that are, in one way or another,
proper to poetry. The first is the lyric situation, which was described
earlier as the oral situation: that in which the subject of the enunciation
communicates directly with the addressees present, in which the object
of the word is not distinguished from its subject and its addressees, in
which self-expression, address, and narration are mingled, in brief, in
which the "right word" does not *recount* the story but *constitutes* it. The
second aspect consists of a number of conventional poetic devices present in other texts where the situation of communication is the same, and
which we can suppose represent a regular feature of the "poetic style."
Kugel (1981) effectively opposes the idea that it is possible to speak of
biblical "poetry," denouncing the prose-poetry dichotomy on which this
idea seems inevitably based. This argument goes straight to the point I
am trying to make; now I must justify the generic difference I seem to
have adopted.

If I have used traditional terminology, it is while protesting against the
univocal dichotomy it generally implies. "Poetry," here, is the product of
several indices. First of all, there is the word *šîr*, "song," which occurs in
the text itself. The root designates the act as much as its result, the two in
fact forming an inseparable unity. Next, there are formal characteristics,
grammatical and syntactical; they are the product of the situation of
enunciation about which we have already spoken in detail. I will not
define poetry, as Freedman does, by the absence of certain features, such
as the particle of the direct object, but by the presence, the predominance, of discourse in the first and second person. The narrative parts, in
which events are recounted, are not missing. Rather, they are framed by
formulae like "Bless ye Yahweh" that subordinate the narrative of the

past to the celebration of the present. It is these kinds of expressions which are traditionally classified as "lyrical." Yet they do not affect the factual content of the statements; hence, there is no reason whatsoever to depreciate the historical truth of the narrative parts.

Third, there is good reason to study the structure of sentences according to the fragile concepts of poetic language. Hazardous as it may be, the enterprise deserves some amount of consideration, if only to stretch the lyric code to its limits. Of the two conventional poetic devices of antique Hebraic literature at work in the song, parallelism and rhythm, only the first more or less survives translation. It is imperative that the translator, sensitive to the much more powerful homonymy in the original language, do all that is possible to preserve this feature. In this respect it is significant that in the different translations I consulted, the texts of chapter 5 are clearly more divergent than those of chapter 4. The interpreter who would be guided in his task by the lyric code has nothing left, then, but traces of the first device.

The concept of parallelism, principal object of Kugel's study, as well as of Berlin's (1985), is as uncertain as it is crucial for the study of the biblical text. Interest in parallel structures has brought forth an abundant literature, most often inspired by the futile desire to categorize them. The opposition drawn between synonymic and antithetical parallelism, sometimes significant, becomes extremely reductive from the moment it is established *a priori* (Kugel 1981:13). What parallel structures have in common is more significant than what distinguishes them. They are dual. The second part, which by definition comes after the first, exploits its position *after the fact.* Linked to the first, it responds to it in a thousand different ways, sharpening some aspect of the first that warrants attention. It enhances or emphasizes this aspect. The relation can be one of definition, of particularization, of accentuation, of opposition, of who knows what else; this is not what concerns us here (Kugel 1981:8). Often, the relation is more clearly expressed by the adverbial "furthermore," but sometimes it is simply additive. This structure is not exclusively poetic, however, nor could it be, given that the category of "poetry" is itself questionable. Nevertheless, the examination of a few parallelisms in the two versions reveals some interesting differences.

Comparing verses 5:26 and 4:21, Kugel (1981:43) puts his finger on a difference that he refrains from explaining.

> 5:26 Her hand she stretched out to the tent peg
>   and her right hand to the workmen's hammer

becomes

> 4:21 and Jael woman of Heber took a tent peg and seized the hammer
> · in her hand.

Both parallelisms, these structures are subtly different. In 5:26, the verb is not repeated, while "right hand" seems to reiterate "hand." In 4:21, "seized" repeats "took," but the hand intervenes only once. The difference is not, therefore, formal. According to Kugel, it is the relation *after the fact* that has changed. In 5:26 it is impossible to know if both hands act at the same time or not; to put it another way, if there is one weapon or two. If read in the sense of "furthermore," the second statement could represent a qualification of the first. In 4:21, the choice is made, the ambiguity has disappeared. The actions succeed each other "logically." There is the difference: the ambiguity of "furthermore" is replaced by the univocal but logical "then." As a result, the whole point of the parallelism has disappeared, and it becomes a simple temporal succession. Taking a closer look, we might say that "logic" weakens the parallelism as such: the subject of action is not the same. If we see the hands at work in 5:26, thus emphasizing the aspect of labor, the "manual" aspect, the narrative defines the murderess in terms of her identification with a group or an individual, thereby emphasizing the political importance of the episode. The parallel structure as Kugel defines it functions fully in 5, where the right hand is a specification of the hand of the first part, while the "workmen's hammer" is added to the nail. Two specifications then, retrospectively, add meaning to the first part, which thereby receives after the fact a more immediately concrete character. There is nothing of this in 4:21, where the succession serves precisely to separate, for purposes of chronology, the different phases of the action. Judging from this example, Kugel is right and wrong at the same time. He is right insofar as parallelism in itself does not, in fact, distinguish the two versions. He is wrong in underestimating the difference in the *degree of expressivity* of the two structures, linked to the form of parallelism itself.

In his crusade against preconceived categories, Kugel disposes a little too easily of another distinction, of great importance for our discussion, between binary parallelism and ternary structure (1981:52). It seems to me he thus eliminates a feature that is precisely characteristic of Judges 5 and other songs as well. The importance of the formal difference is indeed limited, but form, it has often been said, never comes alone. The difference must be seen in light of the frequency of representation in general (Genette 1972b).

There are thus, let us say, two figures: synonymic parallels or repetitions, and climactic parallels or ascending progressions, both to be distinguished from singular representations. The lyric code permits an inventory of phenomena by classification according to three quantities and frequencies (Table 1): singular representation presents *one* element *once;* repetition presents *one* element *twice;* representation in ascending progression presents *two or more* elements *three times.* The sense of "furthermore" in the binary structure yields to an effect of intensification, power-

Table 1

number of elements represented \ number of representations	1×	2×	3×
1	singular representation "it happened"	repetition "furthermore"	
2			ascending progression
>2			ascending progression

ful in a different way, in the ternary structure. In the former, repetition after the fact doubles the effect of the first part. In the latter, the same thing happens, but then the third part will most often intervene to frustrate interaction between the first two by introducing a climactic point, a contradiction, or an ambiguity. The lyric code thus schematized leads to the hypothetical distribution of semantic accents. The elements added in the third restatement are significant: even while remaining homogeneous with the isotopy of the figure, they may give a different nuance to the repeated motif. The lyric code that adopts this principle would propose that elements represented in climactic parallelism are the most important for the thematics of the poem. We can still—and with still more hesitation—suppose that, in the series of semantic elements thus formed, the ascending progression as structuring principle continues to operate. We can now see how the interpretation of the embroidered cloth at the end of the poem, proposed with the aid of the anthropological code, is sustained by the lyric code. The third part or, to be more precise, its end, intervenes ironically to invert the climax constructed by means of gradation: dyed cloth; embroidered dyed cloth—still more precious; twice-embroidered dyed cloth—and then? The answer to the question provoked by the suspense inverts the values: "for his neck," that is, ornamental, or for the vulnerable part of his head, to serve as ashen sackcloth, nonembroidered, noncolored symbol of mourning rather than joy, humiliation rather than glory.

The ternary structure of the last stanza of the song takes us still further. Here, ironic inversion is interdiscursively meaningful. The tradition of victory songs sung by the women is rendered doubly ironic (Globe 1974:498). First, the women would ordinarily come out to welcome the war hero, whereas here they are confined behind the lattice. Next, these women are not singing at all; they are worrying. Deborah, on the other hand, sings, but not, as tradition would have it, to celebrate the victory of others. She celebrates her own, showing not only that women can be active in military matters, but also how far all the levels of the action are intermingled. More and more we understand what interests prompted the "oblivion" into which this stanza was cast in the narrative, and its condemnation by the critics. But to condemn the last stanza because it does not end the poem at its climax plainly makes use of the literary code without knowing how to wield its anthropological counterpart; a shortcoming that has its repercussions for a *literary* evaluation of the poem. As there is no ternary parallelism in chapter 4, the hypothesis that it is a characteristic of the song appears to be justified. Thus the lyric code, as provisional as its status may be, contributes to the furthering of the specificity of each version.

With the help of the lyric code thus constructed, verses 26 and 27 of the song take on a meaning that, if clear, is hardly reassuring. Three phases of the event are recounted in sequence: the preparation, the murder, and the result. The first phase, double, is recounted once, in binary parallelism. The second, the murder itself, is represented either twice in synonymic parallelism, or three times, in climactic progression. For the four verbs can be considered as two series of two, or the first two verbs can be understood apart from the second two. The very structure is thus ambiguous. The result is stressed by the "detail" added in the final position: annihilation. Verse 27 is similarly complex: three synonyms of the fall; then two more, of which the first verb repeats verbatim the very first synonym; then three more, the last of which gives the result. I will return to this elaborate figure; at this point we need only agree that the lyric form here has a power that cannot be ignored. If it is tempting, for some, to privilege the form as a way to evacuate the content, then it is equally plausible to affirm, as we do willingly before more joyous and lofty verse, that the poetess knew exactly how to exploit the specific lyric form to enhance—impressively, it cannot be denied—the agony of the enemy and his definitive annihilation. Compared to this powerful representation, the prose version seems tame, almost innocent. Not only is the description of the death singular as well as simple; not only does Sisera's sleep soften his agony—and excuse his lack of vigilance—but in addition, the other thematic line is immediately resumed, and Barak enters the scene to consummate his shame.

If the presence and absence of the ternary structure is an important difference, the effect in both cases is extremely powerful. The form called "lyric" leads to the harrowing evocation of Sisera's horrible demise. In contrast, the narrative reassures by the uninterrupted introduction of new facts, which leaves little room for repetition. The facts considered "absolutely essential" by Gerleman, the preliminaries of the murder, indeed seem to be indispensable to reassure; even if their insertion means the suppression of a poetic form at the source of an entire creative vision.

The Narratological Code

Generically specific, the code that considers the activity of narration, the structure of the narrative, and the person of the narrator, as a rule of correlation between expression and content, will be called here the narratological code. Like other codes, it can be used judiciously or injudiciously, to open or close the interpretation, to oppose or support other codes, to impoverish or enrich the thematic universe of a text.

Seeking to establish a narrative structure for the prose version, D. F. Murray manipulates the narratological species of the literary code in both its positive and negative aspects. After establishing a structure based on an interaction of linguistic and physical acts (unnecessarily claimed, in opposition to Nathhorst 1970, to be the only structure possible [1979:162]), the commentary continues regarding verses 17–21: "The narrator introduces circumstantial detail, 'trivial' incidents which at once give a vivid reality to the action, and postpone the anticipated climax" (165). It is true that in comparison with the song, the scene seems prolonged.

Considered "trivial," the "details" concerning Sisera's arrival are then attributed to what Barthes calls an "effect of the real" (*effet du réel*) (1966). In this mechanism the hierarchy that prizes denotation over connotation is inverted. The first meaning—that is, the "details" themselves—becomes the expression of a second meaning, /reality/. The concept, and the idea upon which it is based, has its origins in realist literature, where "the little detail which rings true" is esteemed precisely insofar as it is trivial, secondary, and thus capable of signifying something other than the diegesis. Even for this historically and geographically circumscribed literature, the concept betrays the circularity that accompanies all attempts to project interpretive decisions upon a text. For it is the reader, after all, who chooses which diegetical lines are significant and which are not. More important, to call a textual element a detail with an effect of the real is to *exclude it* from diegetical interpretation. In other words, it represents once again the separation of reality and imagination that is part of the historiographic project. The tenacity of this project clearly demonstrates, if we still need convincing, that the interests at stake are weighty—indeed, decisive.

When it determines in advance where the story comes to its dramatic climax, the narratological code becomes even more openly prescriptive, which is to say, restrictive—to the point of censorship. Murray sees that climax in Barak's confrontation with the corpse. The decision can perhaps be justified, although it means censoring the other thematic line, that of deceived hospitality. Details that are circumstantial for the one theme are crucial for the other. What is thus censored, we will see, is, once again, the *critical difference* (Johnson 1980), the differentiation of perspectives according to the sex of the speaker. We have seen how Alonso Schökel, in much more pronounced fashion, used the narratological code to discredit the literary value of the narrative, by grafting it onto the predominant historical code: it is *because* thematics can be nothing but historical that the climax must be the battle, and *because* this is so, the climax comes too soon.

The narratological code can also open up interpretation. If we carefully consider each locutionary act of narrative type in the texts, we are in a position to compare narrative statements with imbedded dramatic enunciations. We could then follow closely, for example, the momentary inversion of power roles between Jael and Sisera, reestablished by nonverbal acts. If Jael takes the initiative in inviting Sisera into the tent, the latter, having entered, takes his own in turn. He makes a request that, once satisfied, is followed by an order. Jael does not respond verbally but physically, executing Sisera's injunction a little too literally.

The concept of focalization, eminently narratological, here becomes pertinent: the same sign, "no [man]," is interpreted differently depending on the focalizer. One interprets it as /I am not here—I am hiding/ and the other as /he is not a man—I will kill him/. The ambiguity rests on the value, substantive or pronominal, of expressions like *'ên 'îš* and *lō' 'îš*, literally "no man" or "not a man." They are usually considered pronominal, equivalent to /no one/ or /none/. But Hebrew does not have indefinite pronouns. To understand the phrases literally becomes a means, then, of restoring what was an ambiguity of considerable significance, of creating the necessary opening through which to reach the underlying codes. This ambiguity becomes irreducible, and the misunderstanding between the characters, comprehensible. Here is proof, if ever there was, of the validity and linguistic basis of the concept of focalization, which has so often been challenged. This clash between two focalizers represents, on a minature scale, the two utterly and irreversibly different languages that belong to the respective speakers of the two versions. As in the celebrated drawing commented on by Gombrich, it is impossible to see the duck and the rabbit at the same time.

The narratological code can make sense out of the narrative itself, and *a fortiori* of the degree of narrativity. We know that the latter as a whole is connected to the historiographic project. Comparing term for term the two accounts of the murder properly speaking, the differences are, again, striking:

Judges 5:

26. Her hand she stretched out
    to the tent peg
    and her right hand to the
    workmen's hammer
    and she pounded Sisera, she
    crushed his head
    and she shattered and pierced
    his temple.

27. Between her feet, he collapsed,
    he fell, he lay still
    between her feet he collapsed, he
    fell,
    where he collapsed, he fell,
    undone/overcome.

Judges 4:

21. And Jael woman of
    Heber took a tent peg
    and seized the hammer
    in her hand and she
    went to him softly and
    she drove the peg into
    his temple, and it
    penetrated into the
    earth,

    and he was fast asleep
    and he was weary and he
    died.

While trying to be faithful to the Hebrew, I have translated the passages so that the differences stand out as distinctly as possible. The narratological code, in its simplest form, consists in the idea that a narrative is the focalized presentation of a series of events (Bal 1984a, 1985). Starting from there, we can assign importance to the fact that one verse is devoted to the event of the murder in chapter 4, and two verses in chapter 5. The divided structure of chapter 5 differentiates the act itself from its result, which is also given the status of an event. As for frequency, 4:21 presents the event in a sequence of action verbs, with each one making a single appearance. In 5, there are numerous repetitions. The elevated number of action verbs in 4 *atomizes* the event; it becomes one action fractured into a series of smaller actions. The event in chapter 5 is *whole:* those verbs which are not repeated are synonyms.

In the translation, the conjunction *we* was systematically rendered as *and*. The word raises a problem of ambiguity analogous to that caused by the expressions that act as—without *being*—indefinite pronouns. As it is the only common conjunction in Hebrew, it serves there where we would use various conjunctions, but this does not necessarily mean that it has the same value. Furthermore, the choice of the coordinating relation is necessarily arbitrary, or rather, interpretive. Compare my translation (on the left) with that of Dhorme's edition:

Juges 4:21:

et prit Jaël (la) femme de Héber   Mais Jaël, femme de Héber, prit
  un piquet   un piquet de la tente,
et saisit le marteau dans sa main   prit en main le marteau,
et elle s'approcha de lui doucement   vint à la dérobée près de lui et
et elle frappa le piquet dans sa   enfonça dans sa tempe le
  tempe, et il pénétra dans la terre   piquet qui se ficha en terre.
et lui il était profondément endormi   Et lui qui était profondément
et il était épuisé   endormi, épuisé, il mourut.
et il mourut.

Judges 4:21:

And Jael woman of Heber took a   But Jael, woman of Heber, took a
tent peg and seized the hammer in   peg from the tent,
her hand and she went to him   took in hand the hammer,
softly and she drove the peg into   came in secret close to him and
his temple, and it penetrated into   drove in his temples the peg
the earth, and he was fast asleep   which stuck in the earth.
and he was weary and he died.   And he who was fast asleep,
                                            being weary, he died.

If the repetition of the conjunction *we* is understood literally, it will appear that the event is presented as a succession of little events that together constitute the great event. In Dhorme's translation, several aspects of the event are presented as explanations, others as elements of the principal action. Dhorme, it seems, has pushed even further the tendency already present in the Hebrew text to differentiate the narrative from the song. His translation is thus even more rational, even more explanatory and hierarchical than the Hebrew version.

In light of this second comparison, the first acquires new meanings. The conjunction *we,* translated by *and,* is also present in the first verse of the song, although less systematically, and absent in the second. A comparison of the *three* versions—the song, the narrative, and Dhorme's translation of the latter—reveals a progression toward a greater rationalism. But there is more here. The song presents the act itself, in verse 26, as a series of acts, just as the narrative does. The differences occur in the second phase: the result of the act. The narrative presents act and result in the same narrative mode, that is, as a series of small, discrete events. Dhorme's translation makes the series into a sequence of explanatory clauses, clauses that excuse. Indeed, the frequency of *we* justifies up to a point this effort at rationalization. But the song drops the conjunction in this part. The fragment thus assumes a more *descriptive* aspect. I tried to render this aspect by using the imperfect tense here.* The descriptive

---

*"The sun was shining" in French takes the imperfect tense; the imperfect is used to refer to repeated, continuous, or habitual actions of the past, often translated in English by *was* or *were* and the - *ing* ending, or by *would* in the sense of *used to.* It is generally the tense of description in the past.—Trans.

mode is strengthened by complements of place, whose importance we will see later: "between her feet," which is repeated, and then restated in "there where." Apparently the spectacle of the agony of Sisera is important here, an importance that the epic narrator sought to attenuate by replacing it with the *reasons* for the death. Perhaps the conjunction *we* should be included in Freedman's list of particles that occur less frequently in poetry than in prose; but then it would be necessary to interpret this difference. What our fragment does suggest is that the lower frequency of the conjunction is symptomatic of more descriptive evocations, and it would consequently become a general index of evocation. Narration on the one hand, evocation on the other: the distinction suggests a difference of genre that, according to the narratological code, signifies a difference of *vision*. Different visions of the medium of language, of literature, of the event; different visions of the focalizer in the technical sense. The lyric focalizer revels in the spectacle of the agony of the enemy, with a sadistic pleasure that must have troubled the epic poet. Hence the latter's decision to give the narrative version a focalizer more concerned with *explaining* than with *seeing*. From then on, rational understanding replaces emotive pleasure.

The narratological code thus attempts to grasp the nature of events, or series of events, and of the (logical) relations between the "pearls strung together." To give an idea of such an enterprise on a larger scale, I propose that we briefly consider the *sequel* to the event of the murder, in order to see what, in each case, the concept of a *sequel* means: temporal sequel, logical sequel, sequel to the experience of the poet?

The two sequels have been judged weak by certain critics, powerful by others. We have seen that Murray criticized the structure of the narrative because the end was too delayed. For him, Barak confronting the corpse of his adversary is the high point. The evocation of Sisera's mother was judged to be ill placed in the poem; the end should have been more forceful. Let us try to characterize both sequels without judging them. In the song, the sequel consists in the tragic and ironic evocation of the mother, a last praise of those faithful to Yahweh by way of a conclusion, and the final closing device, "the land had rest forty years." In the narrative, Barak's discovery of the corpse is preceded by his encounter with Jael, recalling hers with Sisera; here again Jael, proceeding toward Barak to greet him, plays upon the "indefinite pronoun" *'ên 'îš:*

> 4:22 And behold, Barak pursuing Sisera, and Jael came out to meet him and said to him: come, and I will show you the man you seek. And he came in to her and behold: Sisera fallen, dead and the peg in his temple.
> 23 And God subdued on that day Jabin, king of Canaan before [in the face of] the sons of Israel.
> 24 And the hand of the sons of Israel bore harder and harder on

Jabin, king of Canaan, until they had exterminated Jabin, king of Canaan.

The sequel to the murder here is its "publication": Jael repeats her manner of humiliating the man by inviting him into her tent. The man who was the nonexistent "no man" in verse 20 will now be revealed in all his nothingness to the man who, earlier (verse 8), had shown himself unworthy of his sex. The true victim of the humiliation here, in fact, is not so much Sisera as Barak; and he himself is the focalizer of his shame. The expression *hinnēh* "behold," thematizes the focalization even while associating the public witness of the scene with this narrative function. The circle grows still larger: from the intimacy of the tent where the event took place, to this confrontation with the true victim of the humiliation, to the public witness without whom there can be no humiliation (by definition public), Jael's act has become a public affair. Jael herself has become the instrument of a greater project. This project is reintroduced in the very last verse, where the reiteration of the sorrows of Jabin, king of Canaan, suffering under the yoke—not of Yahweh but of the sons of Israel—shows clearly for whoever has not yet understood that what are at stake in this version are political and national interests. In this respect, Murray's reservations concerning the narrative structure demonstrate that this critic is a good reader on this point.

The sequel, here, is thus logical as much as chronological. The epic narration situates events in a series structured so as to enhance the principal turning points of the story; this is its task. Skillfully manipulated, the chronology serves to express logical relations. It is *because* Barak enters the scene at the right moment, that is, after Jael's act, that his humiliation can be consummated through that of his enemy. It is also *because* the private act precedes the public act that the first can be subordinated to the second. The composition of the narrative perfectly obeys the laws of the genre, themselves dictated in turn by the laws of historiography. Here there is no delay of action, only a methodical positioning of each element where it best serves the interest of this grand project.

The points of interest are distributed differently in the song, as we have already seen. The episode in which Sisera's mother does *not yet* consummate her loss brings out the gravity of the enemy's annihilation and the pleasure, perfectly symmetrical, of the victorious. The sequel, here, is an ironic reflection, an inversion, of the preceding scene. There is a semantic link, but it is not "logical," that is, chronological or explanatory. If there is a chronology here, it lies in the joyous experience of the poetess. What is represented is the pleasure of the focalization, a contemplative pleasure that deserves progressive, repetitive, extended representation. Certainly there is also a logic, but it is a different kind of logic.

The end of the song, ascribed to the redactors, nevertheless respects what is at stake throughout the poem. The condemnation of Yahweh's enemies goes hand in hand with the glorification of his believers; the peace of the land, a refrain heard throughout the book but absent in chapter 4, consecrates in fact the occasion of the song-celebration. It does not occur to us, when we read the sequel, to see the act of Jael as the humiliation of one man brought to ruin by the humiliation of another; the humiliation of men does not seem relevant. And what happens to Jabin, king of Canaan, and to the sons of Israel does not seem to interest our poetess.

The Aesthetic Literary Code

After what has preceded, I can be brief concerning the general aesthetic literary code. Besides its generically specific uses, the literary code has its less narrow function. If the abstract object corresponding to the term "narrativity" or, *a fortiori,* "Hebrew lyric poetry" specified to a variable but fairly high degree the range of decodable elements, the object that "literariness" refers to is indefinable. The application of the general literary code will consequently tend to be based on a literary or poetic conception of the Hebrew Bible. Despite the circularity inherent in such a procedure (and similarly implicated in the use of the other codes analyzed), it is possible, nevertheless, to draw from the convergence of various models projected on other biblical texts a poetics of immanence that can then be used as a code.

Starting from different theoretical premises, interpreters like Alter (1981), Sternberg (1984), and Fokkelman (1981) take this approach. Alter and Fokkelman, the first more exclusively than the second, seek to isolate what constitutes, according to them, a poetics of intentional immanence, while Sternberg more openly adopts a modern methodology, even while being careful to avoid anachronism. Alter draws attention to the construction of characters especially by means of verbal or nonverbal actions, which assume a more central meaning where mental actions are not represented and where descriptive discourse is absent (this last feature is perhaps not quite so general as Alter claims it is; as we have just seen, descriptive discourse is predominant in the song). Fokkelman is very attentive—perhaps a little too attentive for my taste—to textual figurations such as oppositions, parallelisms, and cyclical structures. Sternberg, a theoretician of the device called "the combined discourse," relies heavily upon the concept of irony. The three poetics are compatible, specifically literary, and applicable as codes: all establish correlations between textual phenomena and thematic elements.

We have already seen how the historical code, isolating the second episode in order to establish its marginal status, enters into competition with the literary code, which begins with the premise of a cyclical network of masculine characters: Jabin–Barak–Sisera–Barak–Jabin, a structure that differentiates the narrative from the song. The aesthetic principle at work here is the value attached to a structural intricacy, a pretty pattern. As basic to modern aesthetics as ambiguity, this criterion must be considered peculiar to our epoch; all value judgments and all attributions of meaning based upon it represent acts of projection. Only when the results of such an interpretive decision coincide with the findings of other codes can we reasonably attach a value to it that is not anachronistic. This is the price to pay for the autonomist attitude of literary criticism. Far from contradicting the historical code, as these authors suggest, we have seen that the narratological code, just like the more general aesthetic code, ends up confirming its conclusions. The cycle of masculine characters in the narrative proceeds by a zigzagging movement from Canaanites to Israelites, and the principal character, Sisera, represents the turning point between the two others. Murray (1979:170–71) underscores the parallel between Sisera's flight and Barak's pursuit, both on foot, both ultimately converging in Jael's tent, where each finds his utter and devastating disgrace. The philological code is recruited by the literary code when the critic demands, on the basis of this parallel composition, that the word *nas* be translated as /at the same time/ rather than as /now/. The two phrases describing the footrace of the two men begin the same way, and both are invited by Jael into her tent to find there the prize they seek, even if it means losing it at the very moment they obtain it.

The structure proposed on the basis of the literary code opens up the possibilities of interpretations progressively more capable of differentiating the narrative from the song. Once the division between masculine and feminine characters is declared significant, it becomes perfectly legitimate to consider the word "no [man]," which ends verse 20, the order that Sisera gives Jael, as the culminating point of the scene and, given the proposed structure, of the entire narrative. The literary code which tends to favor the concepts of ambiguity, density, and irony, thus upholds the results of the narratological analysis. This positive evaluation functions as a code when it leads to the conclusion that it is in the most dense, ambiguous, ironic places of the text that its semantic center, its message, lies. In this case, the content of the message would concern only men and their masculine qualities: Sisera ceased being a man from the moment he entered the tent, bereft of his chariots and his army, shirking the battle of men against men, giving himself up "into the hand of a woman." The event was predicted by Deborah in verse 9, in an equally ambiguous sentence, where the woman in question is not named. If

Jabin escaped the confrontation by transferring his power to Sisera, Barak did the same in demanding the support of Deborah. At the end of the narrative, there are no men left. Directly or by procuration, they have all been "sold into the hand of women."

If we approach the song in the same way, it becomes clear that this text has a profoundly different structure. We have already seen that the part of the song that describes the murder conforms to the rhythm of ascending progression, a structure that places the accent at the end rather than the center. The theme of dishonor being absent, our full attention is drawn toward the cruel image of Sisera's agony. But, here too, the word that receives all the emphasis in the scene represents the very negation of existence: *undone*. The double thematics of the narrative and the simple thematics of the song converge; they end in the same climax. But they get there by two very different paths. The narrative processes are fundamentally different: if Deborah celebrates the murder in *song*, with the ecstatic pleasure that the victory hymn prescribes, the narrator of the prose version complicates it, envelops it in a complex thematic network in which the irony that is the product of the combined discourse shows the ambiguity that is clearly reflected in the critical reception of the text. The aesthetic literary code introduces here another criterion: the homogeneity of expression and content or *iconicity*. According to this criterion, if the two processes are different, so are their meanings; the annihilation of the man means one thing in the narrative and another in the song. With what we have learned so far we can only guess what this difference is. But we do know it must be tied to all that which, in both versions, surrounds this central notion.

It is often said that whoever uses the literary code incurs the risk of "overinterpreting." To retreat before this risk, however, means to take another: that of closing off the text. The different literary codes all introduce two dangers. Their presuppositions, peculiar to the modern literary experience, tend to force the projection, upon texts that do not lend themselves to it, of categories usually based upon dichotomies. In this case the categories distort the critical perspective. Second, the predilection for opposing literary values to historical reality imposes upon literary exegesis an unnecessarily polemical attitude. Starting with that attitude, it becomes impossible, on the one hand, to understand the place, the function, and the social meaning of texts, and, on the other, to integrate the results of other disciplines. The separation is paralyzing on both sides. In spite of their promising results, even the anthropological codes need to be nourished by a subtle and detailed literary analysis such as only the specialists of the latter discipline are capable of providing. Without such an analysis, the nuances of the imaginary and their relations to reality will be impossible to grasp. In other words: anthropology serves as the bridge between the two domains; even so, the map of the imaginary has to be plotted.

The literary codes are, in another sense, the most daring. The formalist bias with which they begin offers the advantage of proceeding, paradoxically, in a direction away from formalism. For to use form as a code is to say that form has meaning, that it is more than just form. This semantic freighting of formal structures can lead to "overinterpretation," to autonomist arrogance, but also to an understanding of what the words, the discourses, and the imagination are capable of expressing in the narrative or in the song. When we take into account formal and aesthetic choices, it is easier to grasp what *happens,* in the reality of the story, when a poet or a poetess speaks.

We have now seen four different codes at work, each functioning within an academic discipline, all of them capable of exacting an interpretation agreeable to the encompassing institution, all of them able to break this restriction by seeking to acknowledge the texts in their differences, in their otherness. Even if, in practice, the anthropological and literary codes appear more open, much depends upon the institutional restrictions the interpreter allows to be imposed.

·II·

TRANSDISCIPLINARY CODES

If it is possible to consider disciplinary results as founded on specific codes that determine the bias of the disciplines themselves, it is no less certain that numerous interpretations are the product of codes for which no precise disciplinary base can be identified. The results of such interpretations can be found published in all sorts of disciplinary environments, which is an indication of their transdisciplinary character—they are not to be confused with extradisciplinary interpretations, which I do not intend to discuss here. They are published in these environments because a disciplinary institution has recognized them as tied to the discipline, but, in fact, a single article may "belong" to several disciplines: for example, the one that will serve as our paradigm appeared in a journal of biblical philology, but it could just as well have appeared in a journal of literature, psychology, or anthropology. This freedom in regard to the institution, combined with a certain recognition by the latter, is the first feature characteristic of a transdisciplinary code.

The second feature is its unifying orientation. Indeed, devoid of a bias projected by any specific discipline, transdisciplinary codes are guided by a presupposition that reigns equally within disciplines but that is here the fundamental bias: the postulate of unity. Projecting onto a text the desire to unify his/her own concerns, the transdisciplinary interpreter is most often forced to accomplish what Eco, following Peirce, would call an *abductive leap*. In such a "leap," the interpreter declares relevant a rule of signifying correlation, in other words a code, whose relevance is precisely not (yet) clear. It accomplishes the transition from undercoding to coding. The impact of these interpretive acts is enormous: they broaden the accessible semantic domain.

An adopted rule of correlation first assumes a thematic form. On the basis of an *idea* imagined to be the semantic skeleton of the text, the latter is then interpreted as the complex figuration of this theme, this idea. So prominent is this feature of the transdisciplinary codes that I call them *thematic codes*. In the following pages, I will analyze an example of one such code, but it is easy to find others; most interesting are ideological codes, which establish a thematic code on the basis of a particular world view. For example, the Marxist interpreter will establish, out of his philosophical notions, the material isotopy as the pertinent theme determining which textual elements will be selected and interpreted.

Contrary to these so-called thematic codes, another group of codes must be distinguished, which, if equally transdisciplinary, are biased less by an interest in thematic unity than by a presupposition of differentiation. Opposed to the centripetal tendency of the disciplinary and thematic codes, and starting from the proposition that the differential character of every culture, hence, of every text, exerts an irresistible hold upon the consciousness, interpreters who follow these codes will seek to differentiate textual elements in order to follow their figurations.

Within feminist studies, two types of codes at work can be distinguished: the thematic code, when a theme relevant to the relations between the sexes is used as a code, such as love, maternity, or the division of labor; and the differential code, when sexual difference serves as the point of departure for a fracturing interpretation, an interpretation that will bring out into the open the contradictions within a text attributable to a gendered plurality of voices or focalizations. This code is distinct from the thematic code in its tendency to appeal, as it searches for differences, to different disciplines at precise moments of the analysis. It consciously makes itself *interdisciplinary*.

In order to facilitate the comparison, I will treat one instance of each type of transdisciplinary code, each concerned with the same semantic domain: for the thematic code, the example will be a sexual interpretation; for the differential code, a gendered reading that specifies according to the division of the sexes. I will show that the first—censored as much by the presupposition of unity that dominates it as by a gender code that remains implicit (and probably unconscious)—tends to mitigate the differences between the two versions, while the second opens itself not only to differences but, by this very attitude, to diverse disciplines separately invoked.

·5·

THE THEMATIC CODE

Often put to work within the literary code but found elsewhere as well, the thematic code is clearly distinct from the literary codes we have analyzed. It is biased neither by a formal search for the specific poetic elements of a text nor by generic conventions, nor by any single-minded disciplinary effort at reconstruction, whether of the past (historical code), of the religion (theological code), or of the culture's way of life (anthropological code). Its base, *semantic*, resides in a presupposition of unity that reigns in all the disciplines discussed and, no doubt, in many others; we may well wonder if it is not inherent in our very semiotic competence. It stands in horror of contradiction, but it is capable of subsuming opposites.

This presupposition of unity is used as a code when an interpreter seeks to subsume all textual elements under a unified and most often preestablished thematic heading. Often it will be drawn from the tradition in which the text in question is rooted. Because of this, the thematic code is not inclined toward criticism. In addition, it easily becomes ethnocentric when it draws its directing theme not from the text but from the mind of the critic. This is the case when critics biased by a persuasive religious or ideological project, such as priests, pastors, or rabbis, use biblical texts as support for their own brand of truth. Opposed to this ethnocentric tendency stands the idealizing thematic code. The tradition of a text, or what is considered as such, is as if by definition considered *superior* to that of the critic who is summoned to "return to the sources." Curiously, the two opposing tendencies sometimes meet. We have seen this phenomenon in theological discussion, where the theology of the song was sacrificed for the result of "progress," while that of the narrative was presented as exemplary and superior to modern indifference.

Without being conservative by definition, the thematic code is doubly centripetal: it attempts to interpret textual elements and different texts according to a unified theme. Guided by a more general cultural interest, the thematic code offers the advantage of bringing out the semantic kinship of different texts. It distinguishes itself from the historical and theological codes in the way it opens up the thematic field to domains less institutionalized than politics or official religion. It tends to take an interest in the themes, among others, of individual life, which, if again institutionalized in the culture, nevertheless often conserve the traces of their subversion. Examples of such themes are /the younger brother more cunning than the older/ or /the good Samaritan/. The thematic code is to be distinguished from the anthropological code by a lack of interest in underlying reality, and from the literary code by a lack of interest in form, or by the subordination of form to thematic content.

The thematic code can be found functioning in the context of other codes, where it will sometimes even assume the dominant position; such is the case in a certain type of Marxist analysis that, focusing upon modes of production, proceeds to make of them the fundamental theme of a text; or in an interpretation in the framework of the theology of liberation, which adopts the thematic code to subsume semantic elements under this larger theme. Certain structuralist works appear to be built upon the thematic code, as, for example, Leach's study (1983:33–66) on the theme of /sister-mother-spouse/ in the Judeo-Christian tradition. Leach's works, like those of Lévi-Strauss which inspired them, have their place in the institutionalized discipline of anthropology. As the mythocritical branch is less anchored in materiality than other anthropological fields, it tends to become more autonomous. The thematic code will in that case be the most obvious code to invoke.

Closing or Opening of Thematics

In 1985 a special issue of the review *Poétique* appeared, entitled "Du thème en Littérature." The issue is presented as an attempt to reintegrate the studies of content, which had fallen into neglect under the influence of structuralism. The introduction shows that this enterprise is a strongly regressive one: the aim is not, in the end, to transcend the dichotomy of form and content, but simply to return to content. The spirit of the issue betrays itself in formulas like "autonomous discipline *of* themes." Such a formula implies that it would be possible and desirable to itemize and categorize literary themes; and to itemize themes it is necessary to believe in their existence as transhistorical objects, solidly anchored in reality. Such a conviction holds decisive consequences for the attitude to be taken toward texts. To believe in themes is already to go in search of them, to try to identify them in a text; they are there, and the critic has no choice but to expose them.

This attitude in no way transcends the objectivism of the prestructuralist era. It is not, however, inherent in thematics. This enterprise, too, can be regarded as dynamic, as the analysis of the process that consists in *making us believe in* themes. Thematic criticism then constitutes its own object. When it presents certain semantic elements as *the* theme of a text, this meaning thereby comes to predominate over all other possible meanings. The Bible is an important and frequent site of such semantic monopolization. Do not Genesis 2 and 3 tell the story of the corruption of the woman, of the eternal feminine, which brings about the fall of the man? This "theme" is none other than a reaction, which arose at a specific moment in the reading of the text and is the necessary consequence of taking a definitive stand in the war of the sexes; it has no connection whatsoever, logical or linguistic, with the meaning of the creation myth as it appears when considered within the tradition to which it belongs (see Bal 1987).

Thematics defines itself as the search for the answer to the question "What is it about?". It is a semantic enterprise. It should not stop there, however, lest it risk being nothing more than the regression inspired by the nostalgia for certainty that was at the source of the issue of *Poétique*. The following example may illustrate my point. "What is it about?" ask the collaborators of Pierre Bourdieu (1979), submitting, in the disciplinary framework of empirical sociocriticism, a photograph of the hands of an old working-class woman. "Oh, what beautiful hands!" exclaims the worker. "Oh, what a beautiful photograph!" cries the intellectual. Conclusion? Is the worker more endowed with "practical sense"? Is he indeed a beautiful brute à la Zola, as Bourdieu suggests in certain passages? Is the intellectual more endowed with aesthetic refinement? Or does, in fact, the aesthetic formalism of the second reveal an elitist escape characteristic of the bourgeoisie, who turn away from reality in order to avoid seeing its contradictions?

The example is revealing for several reasons. Is it really possible to say that the worker has better interpreted the theme of the photograph? For him, this theme is the hands, including their beauty. For the other, the theme *is* beauty, including its means of expression, the photograph. For the second, the theme is "metatextual." Both reactions seek to account for *what is seen*, for the *object* of the sign—thus, for its semantics—without describing, for example, its details, its functioning, its syntax, its realism, or its rhetoric. They are both thematic insofar as they summarize this object. They designate by a symbolic relation not the entity itself, the "photograph" that the researcher holds in his/her hands, but the hands represented in the work of art. They select the content proper to the *habitus* of the respondent, to his/her ideological reference, to his/her existence.

The example shows that if there is a theme here, it is not definable except in context. It is biased by interests, determined by the reader/spectator. The theme indicated by each respondent is at the same time an aesthetic manifesto. The thematics of "labor," which ties the concept of beauty to visible traces of work, belongs at first glance to a realist aesthetic, which would make the "metatextual" theme of the intellectual something closer to formalism. For the latter, narcissistic self-referential thematics is the counterpart, at the level of the artistic work, of the formalist attitude. The worker, however, displays the same narcissism. For him, traces of labor constitute beauty, in other words, the traces of his own life, just as, for the professional of "pure beauty," beauty itself is central, and thus constitutes *the interest* of the work. By this concept of textual narcissism, the opposition between realism and formalism loses whatever sense it still had.

This example teaches us that thematic analysis cannot distance itself from the personal thematic code of each reader unless it analyzes the process by which thematic reading emphasizes the *center of interest* in a text. The center of interest can proceed only from an interest; it will never be the "reification" of a theme, self-evident, transhistorical. Let us take the example of *cuckoldry*, often invoked to support the transhistorical and ontological status of themes. The example is well chosen. There have been stories of conjugal infidelity ever since the institution of marriage became commonplace (which is already not the same as having existed everywhere and always). But the "theme of cuckoldry" is in fact the sum of only half its stories: those where the woman is "unfaithful" and the man is the victim—the cuckold. Now, it seems to me that the choice of this example typifies the attitude of the thematician-reader before the vast set of possible thematizations. It is the reader who declares that there is a significant distinction between "stories of the conjugal infidelity of women" and the others, even if it means eclipsing the second group. The interest that determines this choice is obvious; it is that interest, and its interaction with texts, which thematics should study.

The questionable character of the thematic code proceeds from a combination of positivism and unification. Positivism would have us believe in the stability of what is not stable; the consequence is an ahistorical methodology. The unifying tendency reinforces this consequence: it allows all differential nuances to be eclipsed. We will see that thematic practice does everything it can to discourage the metathematic analysis that would explain the thematic process.

The Theme as Starting Point

Given the great number of available themes in the stock of a culture, the thematic code will have to be analyzed in the study of a specific case. An illustrative example is an article by Yair Zakovitch that interprets Judges 4 and 5, published in the disciplinary context of the *Zeitschrift für die Alttestamentliche Wissenschaft*. Given the context, the theme could not have been imposed in advance. The analysis is exemplary in several respects. The method is presented explicitly, and the intertextual as well as intratextual elements invoked as evidence are numerous. The analysis concentrates on the scene of the murder in both versions. Thanks to the explicit character of the analysis, it is easy to follow the way in which the thematic approach functions as a code.

Starting with the acknowledged differences between the two versions of the murder, the author affirms from the beginning of his article his intention to demonstrate "dass sowohl in der Prosäerzahlung wie in der dichterischen Darstellung Sissera seinen Tod im Bette des Jael findet" (that as much in the prose narrative as in the poetic representation Sissera finds his death in the bed of Jael). Thus he lays down the sexual theme *a priori*. His choice determined mine: it seemed to me that the sexual theme offers certain advantages too valuable to leave unexploited. First, this theme facilitates the comparison with the gender code. We may wonder to what extent the two codes concur. I will return to this question. Second, the choice of the sexual theme implies taking a stand outside of any discipline. This extradisciplinary aspect makes it possible to see how the thematic metatext fits neatly into the disciplinary context of a journal without making the least concession to disciplinarianism. Only psychoanalysis would have been able to provide a disciplinary context. The thematician's decision to refrain from this possible assistance seems significant to me. On the one hand, it shows the freedom relative to the disciplines that the thematic code seems able to allow itself. On the other hand, it also liberates the thematician from a restriction that would have been profitable to his enterprise. For with respect to gender, psychoanalysis is a differential discipline. To adopt it would have obliged the thematician to differentiate more than he does. Third, the choice of the sexual theme suggests a decision to address meanings less openly proclaimed than those ordinarily accepted. It also implies a particular semantic conception. The type of opposition such an analysis will encounter will prove to be fatally linked to this aspect. Unable to acknowledge that the theme itself must be censored, the critic will declare openly, and paradoxically, that "the theme *is not in* the text."

Immediately after the enunciation of the selected theme, the critic declares the differences between the versions irrelevant, because they are due to censorship:

> Beide Schilderungen stellen zwei verscheidene Stufen von Versuchen dar, diese ursprüngliche Tradition zu vertuschen, nach der Sissera seinen Tod im Schlafe fand, und zwar nach dem Sexualakt mit Jael in ihrem Bette. (1981:365)

> Both descriptions represent two different stages of the attempt to conceal this primitive [original] tradition, according to which Sissera finds his death in sleep, that is, after the sexual act with Jael, in her bed.

The supposed censorship is explained by the desire to protect the honor of Jael and of Yahweh.

The *starting points* thus formulated seem homologous to the *conclusions* to which the disciplinary codes lead; that is, they have the form of theses. The thematic code proceeds inversely. The general sense is fixed in advance. The hermeneutic process consists in projecting this theme onto the details of a text; those details which reflect the selected theme are enhanced. The theme biases the interpretation just as the disciplinary codes did. To put it another way, the arguments, more than the conclusions, constitute the interpretation. Despite an obvious circularity here, let us not dismiss such a procedure too quickly.

The method to be followed is stated explicitly:

> Wir wollen versuchen, diese Annahme zu beweisen, sowohl durch die Analyse der Ausdruckweise in den beiden Traditionen wie auch durch eine Vergleichung dieser Traditionen mit den Entwicklungen der Jael-Sissera-Traditionen in der rabbinischen Literatur sowie mit parallelen Episoden und Situationen in Erzählung und Poesie der Bibel und der apokriphen Schriften, die ebenfalls abschwächende Überarbeitungen erfuhren. (365)

> We will attempt to prove this hypothesis, as much through the analysis of the expressions in both traditions as through the comparison of this tradition with the evolution of the Jael-Sisera tradition in rabbinical literature as with the parallel episodes and situation in the narrative and poetry of the Bible and the Apocrypha, which likewise have suffered attenuating revisions.

The interest of this example for a discussion of codes lies in the identification of the theme—a content—as a rule of correlation between the signs—*Ausdruckweise*—and their specific contents as well as other possible contents; or in other words as an instrument of closure and opening. The case is all the more illustrative because the author openly proclaims his intention to subvert the censorship practiced in the text.

The Thematic Code at Work

The ambiguous verbs in the description of Sisera's death in the lyric version constitute one of the arguments put forward to substantiate the sexual theme. The verb *kāra'*, translated "he sinks," "he sags," or, in the Jerusalem translation, "il s'est écroulé" (he fell, he collapsed), lends itself to speculations of all sorts, for it figures in greatly diverse contexts. /To bend/, /to kneel down/ is said of an animal preparing for sleep (Gen. 49:9) and of a man about to say his prayers (Ps. 22:30); it therefore signifies either relaxation or respect. It also denotes submission, weakness, and subjection. A man can bend down over a woman to subject her to sexual acts, with or without her consent. A woman can bend down to give birth (1 Sam. 4:19). The verb therefore signifies release, an action accomplished or sustained, voluntary or involuntary. The choice made by the French translators ("il s'affaissa") accentuates powerlessness. The choice between an active or a passive event implies an attitude toward the ternary structure in which the verb is inserted, and which is conceived as either synonymic or progressive. Zakovitch thus has the lyric code on his side: the ternary form suggests progression rather than repetition, especially since the figure is in turn the first element of a larger ternary structure—itself clearly a progression—in which it is embedded.

Zakovitch's own lack of precision is a form of self-censorship. He evades saying exactly what the sexual meaning consists in. Trying to find arguments in his favor, we can suppose that, according to the lyric code, the three verbs, "collapsed," "fell," "lay down," form a *chronological* series, representing the successive phases of orgasm: the first signifies the orgasm itself, while the moment immediately afterwards is expressed by "to fall"; the third verb, "to lie down," would then express the post-orgasmic rest here equivalent to death. Those who translate synonymically, on the other hand, represent three times a slackening, thus censoring, along with the lyric procedure, the dynamic perspective, the detailed description of the event—a narrative mechanism—and its possible sexual connotations.

Zakovitch does not draw his argument from this kind of lexicological analysis. Without specifying these meanings, he draws it from the rabbinical commentaries. The Talmud, which according to Zakovitch is in general concerned with enhancing sacred meanings—hence, which represents another kind of thematic reading—in plain language favors the sexual interpretation. The argument has at most a limited value. It ignores the ideological mutations that took place between the two writings, that of the text-source and that of the rabbinical commentary. What is more, the rabbis worked with a conception of the rules of the interpretive game that was very different from ours. They elaborated their theology *around* the text, rather than *on the basis* of the text. Moreover, the metaphorical code they used—and which persuasive interpreters still use today—precludes the application of their interpretations as arguments, such interpretations by definition being unverifiable.

A second argument submitted is the omission, in eighteen Hebrew manuscripts, of the first part of verse 27 of the song. In the commentary of the *Biblica Hebraica* it is suggested that this shorter version could be the original, the repetition being the result of an error called *dittography*. This hardly seems plausible, because the lyric form would thereby be affected, and the verse would then be exceptional in its structure: a parallelism in triple progession. We can just as well, along with Zakovitch, invert this perspective. The state of the verse in the eighteen manuscripts must then be declared an omission due to *homoeoteleuton*. The arbitrariness of the application of these philological terms demands additional corroboration. The argument in favor of Zakovitch's hypothesis—an act of censorship—is supported by that drawn from the lyric code. We notice that the literary codes are indispensable in cases like these. On the other hand, the hypothesis of dittography is no doubt implicitly supported by an underlying, unconscious gender code: the cruel evocation of the agony of the man killed by a woman is painful; its effect is visible everywhere in the commentaries. It is so painful that it becomes inadmissible.

The hypothesis of censorship at this precise point of the text seems plausible to me. Two problems remain, however, which the thematic code leaves unresolved. The first is, again, the motives behind this censorship. If it was meant simply to obliterate the sexual meaning, as Zakovitch suggests, it was not very effective, since the rest of the verse retains the censored verbs. This is why it is necessary to be more specific. For the concept /sexual meaning/ deserves to be differentiated: which sexual events were represented and then censored—and why? Which *aspects* of these events were enhanced or suppressed—and why? And especially: which gender-specific position determined these decisions? The gender code will have to respond to these questions. But let us not jump ahead too quickly. We could argue here that in the repetition, it is not only the *meaning* of the sexual act that is expressed, but also its chronology and its rhythm. This acoustic iconicity, which is particularly perceptible (being an audible phenomenon) in the oral performance, would have begun little by little to disturb later listeners. They were more sensitized to the prudery that is part of the anti-Baalist ideology. We have seen what interests were at stake in this transition from polytheism to monotheism and, more specifically, the relationships between religion, politics, and sexual morality that played a predominant role. The influence of this transition on the censoring of the first element of the tricolon in verse 27 remains uncertain. Even so, it is substantiated by the evidence in Judges 4, which shows that this propriety became stricter as the establishment of the people in the land progressed.

The second problem is that of difference. Only the song has retained those expressions declared ambiguous as much by the modern critic as by the talmudic interpreters. As the author takes the thematics of the two versions to be identical in other respects, one would expect him to explain why the censorship would have been so much more intense in the narrative. Here again, the thematic code does not encourage the critic to specify. It remains indifferent to the song's overwhelming evocation—evocation less of the act of murder than of the victim's agony. If the ambiguity of the verbs suggests that this agony is equivalent to orgasm, the meaning remains double. The desire to make the ambiguous words unambiguous, even in the sense antithetical to tradition, is characteristic of the unifying thematic code. It seems to me more fruitful to leave the ambiguity intact, to adopt it, to let coexisting meanings raise the problem that it is the interpreter's duty to cultivate—since this is his/her garden.* From this point of view, it is the equivalence itself between the height of pleasure and the height of pain, fixed by the ambiguity, which would seem to inspire in the poetess the exaltation to which she gives voice.

The Thematic Code as Censor

Another textual element is brought forward in support of the sexual theme: the milk given in place of the water requested. While water slakes thirst, goat's milk narcotizes, and the effect suggests, once again, censorship: Jael would actually have offered wine, and before making love, the couple would have made merry drinking. The parallel with Judith in particular, but also with Esther, is called upon to reinforce this hypothesis. Whether to sleep or to make love, wine leads us to bed. It would have made Sisera a more easy victim. Here again, the interpretation, suggested by the thematic code, seems quite plausible. I wonder again, then, how the censorship would have been effective, since it appears to be common knowledge that goat's milk has the same soporific effect as wine. Is it not, once again, the thematic critic who censors in spite of himself? He interprets, we might say, according to the rationalist code of the epic version, which prescribes an explanation in the form of an excuse. The wine provides an excuse for the man stupid enough to let himself be duped into so dangerous a situation. The milk, nourishment for children since the beginning of time, has very different connotations indeed. As I see it, it will put the critic above all on the track of another isotopy, compatible with sexuality even while adding another element, less comforting for those who do not recognize its inevitability: the relation between mother and child. Zakovitch, who unabashedly uses the expression "Milch der Jael" (369), "forgets" to cite this isotopy, which emerges out of his own discourse. Once established, even the verbs with double meanings find their semantic potential tripled. I will come back to this in the next chapter. Let us put aside this possibility to consider another example of the sexual meaning.

The first motif Zakovitch submits is the expression *bên ragleyāh,* "between her feet," equally exclusive to the song. The expression is rare in

---

*"We must cultivate our garden": the last sentence of Voltaire's *Candide,* words that have become proverbial in the French language. Candide's injunction puts a greater value on tending to the basic human needs, on setting one's life in order, than on dreams of glory and riches.—TRANS.

the Bible, which is not surprising, given its unambiguous physical precision. In fact, the critic has found only a single occurrence elsewhere, in
Deut. 28:57. Among the abominations that threaten the people—some
of which are literally realized in Judges—the speaker reviles "even her
afterbirth which comes out between her feet." It is thus, in any case, that
the word *šilyātāh*, a *hapax legomenon*, is translated by Osterwald. The word
Aftergeburt is assimilated to the sexual meaning, as much by Zakovitch
(1981:367) as by the rabbis he cites, with a surprising innocence. This is
all the more remarkable since an expression parallel to "between her
feet" intervenes in Judges 16, one of the selected narrative parallels, in
which Delilah holds Samson "between her knees." This expression, less
rare than the other, is elsewhere employed exclusively with reference to
childbirth (Gen. 30:3). The anthropological code as discussed in the
section entitled "The Ethnographic Context" provides the key to the
concrete meaning of the expression, clarifying that the woman gave
birth on her knees, the infant falling between two stones—and between
the feet of the woman. The censorship of the isotopy of maternity is
astonishing, and the thematic code does nothing to prevent it. What
interests determine this censorship, which becomes more and more fla-
grant as the thematic argument proceeds? I will try to answer this pernicious question in the next chapter. Let me only state here that it is a
complex form of censorship, and one that only half succeeds in its task. It
betrays itself in the thematician's symptomatic reading of the two texts.
The desire to unify meaning takes on a more defensive appearance when
the critic finds it necessary to invoke problematic cases to support his
theme. It is nevertheless his choice of theme and his desire to lay bare the
workings of censorship that dictate the choice of his examples. These,
then, put the critic in a difficult situation. Here we have a perfect example of the double nature of codes: they open, they give access, and *by the
same token*, they close. But the meeting of the closing and the opening is a
symptom of the code's own contradictions.

This self-betrayal of the code is visible in a last detail that allows the
critic to disregard the third meaning: the repeated use, in the narrative
only, of the verb "to cover." According to the thematician, the verb is
again evidence of censorship and would have been inserted twice to
suggest innocence: as soon as Jael, out of the bed, puts the blanket
between her and Sisera, the reader would be reassured. I found it difficult to believe in such innocence; the critic himself writes that in the
parallel story of Judith the bed is carefully prepared, and the same verb
appears.

If the critic himself, then, says that the covering can just as well signify
the sexual act—metonymically: before or after—even while attributing it
to censorship, he admits that he himself censors all possible allusion to
maternity. Even so this theme becomes more and more obvious: in the

narrative, the solicitous woman nourishes the man with her milk before covering him in a second time. There is nothing of this in the song, which, on the contrary, offers a violent description, where agony, orgasm, and birth are coextensive. If both texts imply sexual relations between the two characters even while they censor them, the form this description adopts and the possible censorship implied is very different in each case.

The Code as Method

Thanks to Zakovitch's explicit methodological discourse, the thematic code lends itself particularly well to an analysis of the functioning of the method as code, that is, as a rule determining the attribution of meaning. The method announced and meticulously followed in the article consists, we have seen, of three steps. Parallel stories are selected—on the basis of theme—and details that confirm the theme are called upon to support it. Repetitions are explained as cases of censorship, the repeated act being intended to reassure the audience. Ambiguous expressions with sexual connotations are examined. All three procedures are biased by the thematic code, inasmuch as they are all formulated on the basis of a pre-established theme. This circularity is not inevitable; the thematic code permits but does not impose it.

The selection of "parallel" stories, for example, would have been more convincing if it had been based on a different isotopy. A possible coincidence of the sexual theme would have been less circular. One possibility was at least as obvious: the theme of /murder by means of subterfuge/. This theme would have immediately pointed to the preceding chapter of Judges, where Ehud displays a similar kind of subterfuge, and where, besides, the sexual theme deserves consideration. Without even mentioning this case as well as others, the critic presents the stories of Judith, of Esther, and of Delilah as parallel. The last case is interesting; it represents a good point of attack for a critique. For, contrary to the other heroines, Delilah belongs to the enemy camp. This inversion of loyalties goes unnoticed and by the same token suggests what is really at stake in the thematic enterprise. Orienting the interpretation in the direction of unity, the code reinforces a cultural tendency to associate an action like the murder of Sisera with a particular gender. The choice between Ehud and Delilah in the series of parallel murderers is a choice biased by a gendered interest. Zakovitch suggests with just cause that the story of Delilah could very well be the remnants of a Canaanite tradition, and, once the perspective is inverted, it becomes clear that this case, problematic before, now falls back into its proper place. This doesn't make it any less strange that the author chooses it rather than, to give again only the closest example, the story of Ehud, especially considering that Delilah does not actually kill Samson and receives no praise for her act. We can only conclude that the thematic code is here diverted from its project by an underlying parasitic code that is no longer simply moral but gendered. The stories chosen have in common neither the murder nor the paradoxical support given to the Jewish people by a marginal woman. The theme at stake, undisclosed because undisclosable, is that of the /snare of feminine seduction/. Ehud would cut a sorry figure in this company. The modification of the thematic project has its consequences. It permits the thematician to contribute, without saying it and probably without knowing it, to the reification of an ideologeme without justification. Certainly, Zakovitch is not the first to bring grist to this mill. In a sense, we can even say that he does nothing but repeat what the whole tradition of the last centuries has already said. But this is precisely what is most regrettable: the paraphrase of the same old story is essentially undiscriminating, hence, uncritical. The thematic procedure, which gathers in a single heap textual objects whose common characteristics cannot be made explicit, stimulates this uncritical attitude.

As for the other two procedures, there are problems, too. If the repetitions can sometimes be explained by an attempt at censorship, the omissions of repetitions could originate from the same cause. Moreover, the repetitions are not always comparable. For Zakovitch the same principle explains the repetition of "to cover" (4:18, 19) and the repetition of the description of the death of Sisera (5:27), whose omission in the manuscripts he had previously criticized. Thus, the concept of censorship loses its critical force to become an explanatory master key. The two cases are different. The repetition in 4 is *diegetically* functional: it belongs to a whole series of reassuring gestures. In 5, it is *mimetically* functional, representing, perhaps with sadistic pleasure, orgasm, death, and birth in a disturbing equivalence. Here again, even if on another level, unification suppresses the differences. The repetition in 4:18 and 19 contributes to the representation of the murder as a series of little events; it demonstrates the specificity of the narrative as a literary form. In the same way, the repetitive evocation in 5:27 specifies the literary genre. Here, the repeated act of representation itself is the object of the repetition. To treat both of them as cases of censorship is to eliminate the generic differences whose semantic importance we have already seen.

The last observation leads us to a third methodological problem. The critic uses the expression *Nebenbedeutungen* (secondary meanings), which, without being exactly the same as "connotations," is clearly used in the same sense to suggest ambiguity, notably in the verbs of the song. The critic is surprised that the rabbis agree in openly attributing, without ambiguity, sexual meanings to the verbs in question; for according to Zakovitch, the rabbis in general were inclined to sanctify the texts. Now if, under these conditions, the rabbis appear so openly "liberal," there are other ways to explain it. Let us suppose that, if there were grounds for censoring, the rabbis would have joined the enterprise. This they seem not to have done: either they could not do it, or they did it nevertheless, or both. They could not, because the verbs were not ambiguous. Instead they represented cases of "homonymy." Schogt (1984) clearly demonstrates to what extent these semantic categories are difficult to distinguish. In the case of a dead language, the problem is still more pernicious. The hypothesis of a more or less metaphoric homonymy, serving a necessary explanatory function, makes it possible to resolve the problem of Zakovitch's naughty rabbis. The sexual word would have the same form as the other, more "decent" word, but was a different word nevertheless, in the same way that the word côte/littoral (coast) is a different word from côte/os (bone, rib). The rabbis would thus have spoken a language different from that of the text. This language being dead, Zakovitch can no longer understand it (see Eco's appraisal of the "vitelli dei romani" cited in the epigraph). The language here concerned, we have seen, is exclusive to the song. Now the words "come out" in 4:14 come back to mind. We saw that, according to a specific theological code, the phrase could have a sense fundamentally different for Barak than for Deborah: abstract and figurative for the former; concrete, expressive of a cosmic theology for the latter. The same possibility can be suggested here. The language of Deborah would be different, and the words she uses, strongly homonymic. In this case, neither /orgasm/ nor /childbirth (labor)/ would be secondary meanings in respect to /agony/: they would be strictly equivalent. To use terms like *Nebenbedeutungen* or "connotations" here is already to practice censorship: a censorship directed less against sexuality in general than more specifically against the humiliating and harrowing aspect it appears to assume under certain conditions.

Let us assess the methodological value of this code that was selected to represent the centripetal transdisciplinary procedure. It is difficult to escape a negative evaluation. Such an evaluation is forced upon us all the more since the paradigmatic example is an excellent specimen of its genre. Zakovitch is much more explicit than the average thematician, so that it would be unfair to hold this assessment against him personally; I hasten to add that it is the fatal inadequacy of his code rather than the way he uses it that explains this verdict of relative failure. As for the positive side, the thematic code is useful insofar as it offers us the preliminary freedom to begin from any position, its starting point being the *under-coded abduction*. This freedom is indispensable since distant texts whose codes are partially lost always hover in suspense between anachronistic interpretation and incomprehension. The disciplinary contexts that bias the codes derived from them share the disadvantage of being *a priori* limiting; they are also, by necessity, anachronistic. The thematic code is just as limiting, but the theme that directs its interpretation is relatively free, and this, despite the serious disadvantages, facilitates contact with the codes of the text. Without knowing the code, we adopt it, just to see. But once the code is adopted, it is likely to prevent us from seeing, and, in its attempt to defeat censorship, to practice it.

·6·

THE GENDER CODE

So far, each code put to the test has revealed its tendency to unify the two versions of the murder of Sisera. If the differences were sometimes acknowledged, the code in practice mostly served to purge them, not to interpret them. The gender code is summoned to correlate the signs—the problematic differences—to a content—the specificity of the discourse and universe of both sexual groups. Just as with disciplinary codes, notably the theological and literary codes, the meta-gender code adopted by the interpreter in search of difference ought to be distinguished, first, from the personal gender code he or she has also adopted, most often implicitly, by virtue of membership in a particular sexual group, and, second, from the gender code he or she assumes the other has adopted.

The gender code will lead the interpreter to enhance, not to eliminate, the differences between the two versions; it will do this by structuring those differences according to the division between men and women on which the thematic network will be based. The distinction between men and women is thus declared significant; this is the very foundation of the code. Note that I say *distinction* and not *opposition*. The gender code is not *a priori* polemic or dualistic. To keep in mind one sexual group is not to oppose another; it is to see the differences that separate them. To a certain extent, the presupposition of polemic is itself rooted in a sexist ideology, for it proclaims the significance of each sex for the other to be permanent and total. If the present chapter is intended to bring out the concerns of both sexual groups implied in the two texts, it is not necessarily in order to show that the sole object of those concerns is the *other* sex.

The differences can be organized into categories, some of which have already been applied in the interpretations analyzed earlier: the subjects of enunciation and of focalization, diegetical acts and their subjects, the religious vision, the literary genre, the principal theme and its underlying thematic network, tonality and evaluation. These are precisely the themes emphasized by the disciplinary codes. This should not surprise us: the gender code, which is transdisciplinary, depends upon the integration of disciplinary codes. It cannot help but follow some ordering

111

principle. The unifying principle of the thematic code, however, is precluded, since it is upon differences that the gender code fastens. Moreover, the presupposition of a cultural difference between the sexes obliges the code to appeal to specialized disciplines when the examination of different aspects of cultural expression becomes necessary for the analysis. However, in order to avoid the redundancy such a procedure is likely to entail, I will not go so far as to thematize all the appeals to a particular disciplinary code; the readers will have no trouble identifying them. As in certain preceding examples, I will confront the possible contribution of a meta-gender code to the personal gender code, which, as we will see in the sample interpretations, remains implicit.

The Gendered Subject

In general, the narrative of chapter 4, as well as the rest of Judges, is attributed to a male author. There is little reason to doubt this attribution, even if the oral base, which is extremely heterogeneous, does not exclude contributions from feminine traditions. The very existence of Deborah the poetess bears witness to this. The possibility remains, however, that at the period of the drafting even the possible fragments by a feminine author were reworked by the redactors, who were not only males but also probably members of the dominant religious institution (e.g., Mayes 1983). We have seen in the second chapter that this institution was characterized by a progressively intense suppression of all that was considered feminine.

In principle, the situation of chapter 5 is similar. The song of Deborah, whoever its original author may have been, was inserted in the same way into the book of Judges. The same redactors set about adapting it to its surrounding, a form of appropriation that must have left traces. But, as I have already argued, the original orality and the immense popularity of the song can be deemed responsible for its insertion; without its protected status, it would have been alienated to the point of unrecognizability. This is why we are justified in accepting the explicit attribution of the *šir* (song) to a feminine subject. Let us try to imagine what could have happened. First, no doubt, the redactors added the first and last three verses, which represent the cement of the book, to this hypothetical text that circulated in the popular culture and was attributed to a feminine subject. Whether that subject is historical or not, and if she is, to what degree, is less important than the existence, as cultural commodity in circulation, of her text, the text that is attributed as a whole to her.

In addition, the materiality of this object is attested by the archaicism of its language and the specificity of its form. Faced with these facts, and given the lack of evidence pointing to the contrary, one has to be victim of an implicit gender code and personal androcentrist bias to maintain that the feminine subject is only fictive or figurative. The question, from then on, is more revealing than its answer—like the question: Was Joan of Arc a man? The vast majority of critics consulted, regardless of their discipline, seem caught in the trap. Their attitudes vary. Most of them do not even raise the question; they adopt the masculine personal pronoun without further ado. Others (Coogan 1978) satisfy modern American conventions, putting in one "he or she" and then feeling free to continue with the masculine. Still others (Gerleman 1951) attach a masculine subject to a description of his activity as intuitive and irrational; although it is not stated explicitly, what we in fact hear is the implication that these are "primitive" as much as feminine characteristics.

Thus critical discourse integrates ethnocentrism with sexism—an attitude frequent enough in the commentaries. Showing a still more developed awareness of the gender code, Cundall raises the question of the subject of the discourse (1968:91) and concludes that the author was a woman, not without mentioning an interesting philological argument. "Verse 7 in which Deborah speaks in the first person appears conclusive, but most modern scholars (cf RSV) render the verb as a second singular feminine, which is grammatically allowable." This ambiguous verbal form has indeed caused much ink to flow. It seems decisive for reasons that touch on orality. If it were the second singular feminine, we could hypothesize a collective voice, clearly distinct from that of the redactor doing the insertion. The exhortative mode of the song would thus be explained by the presence of the people gathered for the celebration of the combat. The attribution of the rest of the text would thus be extremely vague, and one could pull through with a minimum of text that would *have* to be ascribed to Deborah. But to do this requires that one have the desire to do it in the first place.

From either point of view, the argument, it seems to me, is without any value whatsoever for the issue at stake. If Deborah speaks in the first person, the fact remains that her discourse is embedded (see Bal 1986) in that of the presumed male subject who cites it. In general, embedding is not a conclusive point; the fact, for example, that Sisera's discourse is cited in 4:20 does not prove that the *text* belongs to a male subject. Conversely, if the verb can be translated in the second person, this in no way invalidates the hypothesis of a feminine subject. First of all, self-address in the second person is quite common. Deborah could still be the subject of the exhortation. Next, the oral tradition underlying the text presupposes a situation of enunciation; hence, verse 7, like verse 12, could be attributed to the audience, enthused by the stimulating lyricism of the hymn, and encouraging the singer by stressing the importance of her role. Besides, if the grammatical person is irrelevant as evidence of a feminine subject, according to Van Dijk-Hemmes it remains significant for the ideology of maternity that is expressed here. If Deborah accords herself the title of honor, "a mother in Israel," this title has a meaning radically different from that which the voice of the people might imply, who would seek in her protection from danger—the maternal function in the narrow modern sense, a little saccharine (1983:692). More is at stake in the philological discussion than at first appeared: not only does it suggest that the critic wants to eliminate the possibility of a female subject, but also it imposes upon his analysis the ideologeme of the sweet, caring mother as a cover-up for the threatening image of the female leader. The interpretation of this detail will affect that of the final stanza. Those who translate this verb in the second person are inclined to conceive of the maternity ascribed to Deborah as the sugar-sweet kind. The stanza on Sisera's mother will then be attributed to a "feminine sensibility," with possible indignation expressed at the cruelty of the evocation. No need to fear contradiction here: if the translation of the verbal form liberates the critic from a feminine subject, the relation that is immediately established in the final stanza reintegrates it.

The ambiguity of the verb, in which the second person singular feminine is indeed equivalent to the first person, has never, to my knowledge, been *adopted*. Let us suppose for a moment that the ambiguity, inevitable considering the resemblance of the two forms, did not in any way inconvenience the subject of the enunciation; let us suppose it represented an advantage, something to capitalize on. We may then perceive a play of words, a double meaning that refers to the oral situation and to the theme of the song simultaneously. The purpose of the song is to reunite the tribes in order to celebrate the event *together;* the solidarity of the most remote members, represented by Jael—a woman on the fringe of the people—was decisive but only barely established; not all the tribes participated. Commemorated and commemorating event coincide, thanks to the power of the *right word*. In this celebration of community, the resemblance of the second and first person forms of the verb is the fortunate linguistic peculiarity that allows the poetess to suspend the distinction between the voice that sings and those for whom, *with* whom, it sings, in order to inculcate even more effectively in her audience the value of the community. The honorific title "mother in Israel" falls to the one who is able to produce this beneficial community: the verbal form *I/you arose,* the right word if ever there was one, creates it. The words are rich in meaning in the mouth of the poetess: the verb *to arise* could refer just as much to the military enterprise as to the voice that celebrates it.

At the primary level that is our concern here, the basic interest of this philological discussion lies in the attempt it betrays to abolish the feminine subject. Indeed, as I suggested above, if all the philologically ambiguous cases were systematically translated according to the male gender code, the indices of a feminine subject would no doubt be greatly reduced, but their effect, which is decisive in other ways, would resist elimination. The attempt forces all those who condemn Deborah for primitive and cruel savagery to contradict themselves—like those who, on the contrary, admire her intuition and her feminine sensibility. It is an effort guided by a gendered interest. To so desperately refuse to admit a woman's participation in the production of this cultural, religious, and national book is to acknowledge an inveterate androcentrism; it is to accept the interpretation, which I gave in the second chapter, of the evolution of the religion. Refusing, in turn, to use philology to answer once and for all a question so perfectly and offensively indicative of that interpretation, I choose to leave the technical question of the real subject of the text undecided.

The Gender Code and the Narrative

The subject of the enunciation as it is interpretable from the text is an entirely different matter. I will here defend the thesis that the implied author or interpreted narrator (Booth 1961, Yacobi 1981; cf. Pelc 1971, Bal 1982) of the prose text is masculine, that of the poem feminine—the conclusion itself being less interesting than the arguments called upon to substantiate it. They are first of all based on three issues: diegesis, focalization, and thematics.

As Murray has so effectively demonstrated (1979:188), the epic narrative contains four episodes—five, if one counts the final verse—which represent in descending progression a cycle of masculine characters. Jabin, the king in power, is eclipsed by his general, Sisera. It is thus the military aspect of power that is emphasized. Barak, the leader of the opposing army, begins in a position of uncontested military power but is willing to share it because he does not feel equal to his task. Once Barak's honor is damaged, the attention shifts to Sisera, who sees first his military power and then his personal power reduced to nothing. If Deborah takes it upon herself to inform Barak what he will lose in retreating, what his cowardice will cost him, the task of teaching him his lesson falls to Jael.

The parallels between Sisera's flight and Barak's pursuit, both finding their ultimate defeat in Jael's tent, have already been indicated. Presiding over the destiny of the masculine characters who are ruined, each in turn, for having wanted to shirk their duties, the two women are interchangeable. In verse 9, when Deborah declares that "Yahweh will sell Sisera into the hand of a woman," we do not know if Deborah refers to herself, or to Jael, or to any woman.

The interchangeability of both women is important, it seems to me, for two reasons. First, it makes the two women into a single *category* in which each has her predetermined place. At the same time, prophetic discourse as a rule is ambiguous, by virtue of its function. And it is precisely in chapter 4 that Deborah is presented above all as *prophetess*. The function of poetess, so crucial in the song, has disappeared. Armed with a logic both anachronistic and foreign to the text, Slotki (in Cohen 1980) attempts to dispel this ambiguity:

> The context makes it clear that the reference is to Deborah and not to Jael. Her compliance with his condition will deprive Barak of the glory of the victory. If it were Jael whom she meant, the remark would be pointless, because Jael's part in the enemy's defeat was not dependent on whether the prophetess accompanied Barak or not. (188)

This critic fails to recognize prophecy even when he is confronted with it head on. Ambiguity and inversion of chronology are precisely the distinctive features of prophetic discourse. Deborah is introduced, in verse 4:4, in response to the cries of the oppressed sons of Israel, as a woman, a prophetess. The word woman is here eliminated by the same critic. The inversion of chronology, which is proper in prophetic discourse, requires that gender and function be integrated in the final realization of the prophecy. We can then invert Slotki's argument (and we have good reasons for doing so), and propose that Deborah is here *called* woman prophetess so that in 4:9 she may prophesy in her capacity as woman. The class of woman is at stake, not Deborah the individual; the way the prophecy is realized proves it. Furthermore, Slotki's argument is not valid because the event is presented not as a condition but as a *consequence* of Barak's cowardice. Third, to prophesy is by definition to predict outside the laws of logic; it represents the very disruption of logic.

The conception of the feminine gender as a general category is important for still another reason. Such a category is possible only in terms of a preoccupation exclusive to the masculine gender in societies where the division of labor reserves the military domain for men. For what is at stake here is *the honor-shame opposition, linked to that between the sexes*. This theme happens to be central to the narrative, as it is to many popular stories in the feudal tradition (see Korsten 1985), and up to the present day it figures, in varied forms and with specific historical nuances, in all sorts of cultural artifacts. For this reason it warrants a closer analysis. In the diegesis of our narrative, where life and death are at stake, it assumes a form that makes it stand out even while revealing its psychic origins. Here, honor simply represents existence; shame, annihilation. A more radical expression of the theme is hard to imagine. The ideologeme involved here is thus in force exclusively for men. Significantly, its enunciation is put into the mouth of Deborah, a woman, but the discourse she pronounces is embedded in that of the narrator, whom we have supposed to be a man. The structure of this ideologeme can be represented as in fig. 5.

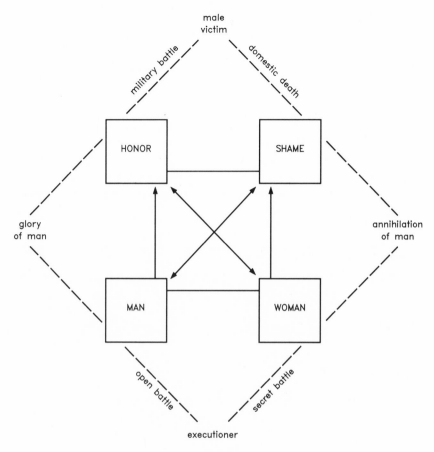

Fig. 5

The expression of this scheme of semantic relationships falls to a woman, and so does its realization. This is not to say that women would agree with it. Here, the narratological code must be appealed to for assistance. With this code we may address the formal structure of the narrative as such, in order to incorporate it in our interpretation. The distinctive feature of the narrative at hand is the structure of embedding. The discourse of a first narrator cites the discourse of another, over which he retains control. Either he selects it, in the case of an entirely documentary narrative, or he invents it, if the narrative is purely fictional. The present case is situated somewhere between these two extremes: the author, informed of the words of the (oral) tradition from which he draws his material, has his delegated narrator "cite" his own interpretation of what tradition attributes to Deborah. Sensitive after the fact to the correspondence between prophecy and realization, he chooses elements he himself judges to be significant. These are the elements that connect the tradition to the theme that is his particular concern: the difficult test of military honor. *It is because they are not subject to the test that the two women, characters portrayed in a man's discourse, are capable of assuming their function in this discourse so distinctly biased by the masculine code.* They are simply not concerned. If Deborah speaks, Barak listens, and assimilates her words; if Jael acts, Barak sees and consummates his shame in that of the other man brought to ruin. If the women execute the scenario, Barak is the focalizer of the shame that is the just reward of the cowardly: of Jabin, of Sisera, of himself. The words of Deborah the woman are cited so that the male addressee can understand the message. The roles are reversed; the subjects of language acts are less important than their objects. The addressee of the word takes over and becomes the focalizer of the result. This can only make the narrative structure more complex: it is not clear, from then on, where the thematic interest lies in relation to the narration. That interest seems to move from actions, strictly speaking, to results; from the narrative to the moral; and from narration to focalization (fig. 6).

Murray (1979:173), receptive to the interchangeability of the two men by virtue of their shame, speaks of "the ignominious subjection to the effective power of a woman." In fact, this effective power lies in the collaboration of two women: together, they work at the task of "subjugating Barak through Sisera" (178). But if Barak, Deborah's friend and perhaps colleague, is the real victim, what is at hand here is no longer a war between two peoples. In the episode that begins at verse 6, and that parallels, in order to subsume it from verse 17 on, the episode of the national war, what transpires is a war between the sexes, or rather, the struggle of one sex against the other. The ideologeme honor/shame effectively demonstrates to what extent the two themes go hand in hand.

The thematic network that crystallizes around this vital question /to be or not to be/ applies exclusively to the masculine subject; the question can thus be translated as /to be a man or not to be a man/. The thematics here are complex and, from the point of view of the gender code, polemic. Honor, equivalent to existence itself, is from the masculine perspective threatened by women. This explains the series of antagonistic couples: Deborah–Barak (4:9), Jael–Sisera (4:17–21), and Jael–Barak (4:22). When Jael presents Barak the body of Sisera, which represents his (Barak's) own shame, she joins them, she makes them interchangeable. Each the enemy of the other, they are inseparable, indistinguishable before the shame represented by the woman as executioner. (For an anthropological study of the relations between honor/shame and women, see Pitt-Rivers, 1976.)

Why should this be so? And why does it provoke such outrage? Here a number of results obtained in the preceding chapters converge. The

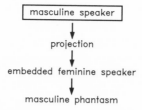

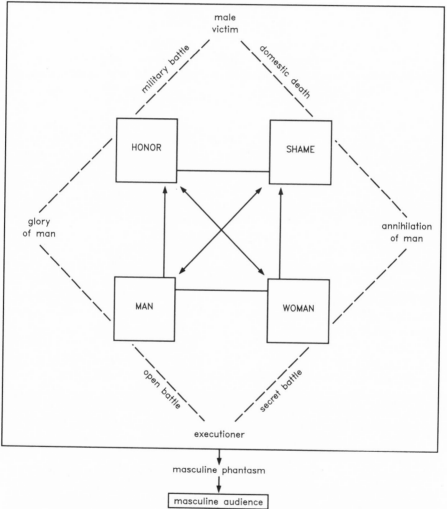

Fig. 6

honor-shame ideologeme represents the nucleus of a social "logic" that is at the source of apologetic and explanatory subthemes. The anthropological code had already shown us the significance of deceived hospitality in ancient Mediterranean cultures, which in turn had been interpreted at a more intimate, domestic level. It is this transition between social laws and personal interaction that seems to be at stake here. Note that the scene of the invitation, like that describing the attentions bestowed upon Sisera in the intimacy of the tent, is absent from the poem, with the exception of the "nursing." Let us see once again what happens, at conscious and unconscious levels alike.

Sisera the commander was defined by his chariots, which, as evidence of his own superior civilization, would have conferred upon him an absolute power if there had not been a collaboration between Deborah and the forces of nature. Once on the ground and off his chariot, he already no longer exists, at least in his official capacity. "To dismount from his chariot" is the equivalent of "to fall from his horse" in the epoch of medieval chivalry (Korsten 1985). It is the dishonorable act *par excellence:* the man is forced to give up the very sign of his superiority, hence, of his identity based upon it. The sign functions by metonymy: local, it connects the man to that upon which he rides, and by means of which he moves about; social, it connects the man to his profession as military leader. Existential, the metonymy becomes synecdochic, because the chariot/horse is part of himself. The shame is all the greater, is *definitive,* because this event, which is only a small incident, betrays the arbitrary and unnatural, because perishable, character of this very superiority. From such a fall one can never recover. Sisera is thus condemned by the ideology of his own class. He now lives for no other reason than to consummate Barak's disgrace, so that the words of the prophetess come to fruition.

Between the moment when he abandons the chariots, when he abdicates his social position, and that when Barak beholds his corpse, Sisera embarks upon a journey that progressively cuts off all means of escape and all freedom of choice. Arriving in front of Jael's tent, he already no longer knows where he is: between the two armies, in an encampment whose status as ally is tenuous, only recently pledged. He is literally lost. The ritual of the invitation from then on holds all the dangers and the ambivalence, but just as much all the urgency, of a *rite of passage.* The ritual is realized outside the tent; once Sisera has entered, it is repeated, at the private level. The social ritual that signifies security according to the rule of hospitality is replaced by another, more dangerous ritual. Now, Sisera is truly alone with the other, stripped not only of his chariots but also of the protection guaranteed by the public domain. He gives himself up to the enemy, but it is not the ordinary enemy. It is the one before whom we are irreparably alone: the state of transition, the central moment of the rite of passage. This danger, this enemy, is represented by the woman. The man who was once so powerful in the superiority of his chariots must now ask for water, the minimal element of survival, from a woman. He gets more than he asks for: he is *nourished.* What Jael offers him are the basic attributes of maternity: protection, rest, and milk. These attributes, which have the power to *restore,* mark the bottom line to which Sisera has descended. He can go no farther: the door is closed upon his public life, upon that existence where honor and the level of civilization counted. The roles are reversed: here, it is the woman who controls, who gives—and who kills. She gives life and then she takes it back.

The reversal of roles, the isolation from society, the regression back to the rudimentary: the elements of the rite of passage (Turner 1981) are all here. It is a harrowing moment—and the capacity to survive the terror inspired by this state of annihilation constitutes precisely the test. That is the criterion which determines the success or failure of the rite. Sisera makes one more attempt to escape it: he commands Jael to stand at the door. This act is decisive. The man in transit, who is nothing but a kind of transient, dispossessed, tries to turn back, to return to the moment when contact with the world was not yet severed. And he tries to return to the moment before the reversal of power roles. He gives an order to the woman who has over him the absolute power that a mother has over her infant. Philologists have observed that the form of the imperative is masculine (*'ămōd*). One could just as well interpret the form as an absolute infinitive (*'ămōd*), which has a strong imperative force (Boling 1975:98). Here again is a philological problem whose ambiguity I prefer to exploit for the benefit of our interpretation. Thus, we protect the text at the same time against the arbitrariness of an unmotivated philological decision and, even worse, against a gendered bias. The contribution of philology should not be rejected; on the contrary. This discipline supplies us with the valuable argument of a possible ambiguity. If this is the case—and how, before an archaic text recognized as enigmatic, could we affirm the contrary?—we can again attempt a reading from two possible points of view. The form of the absolute infinitive, neuter, satisfies the "logical" demands of the more prosaic readers who require that a feminine addressee be properly implied, or at least not excluded. The form of the masculine imperative is superimposed, at the very least by virtue of its audible formal proximity, onto this first "logical" reading. Then it is possible to see in the masculine form a final attempt on Sisera's part to regain his former role as commander: he is accustomed to giving orders to men. The irony of the double sense of the content of his order is only all the more poignant: in this last burst of power, hence of social existence, he pronounces his death sentence, describing himself as "no [man]," and adopting, inappropriately, the discourse of the imperious man he once was.

We have seen, however, that this ritual of hospitality, first social and public, then private and consummated in complete isolation, is accompanied by a second ritual, the (s)election of the sexual partner. The request for water constitutes Sisera's first words upon his entrance into the episode. The request as a speech act has a specific linguistic and psychoanalytic sense. From the linguistic perspective, one cannot significantly request unless one lacks something, and when the addressee is theoretically in a position to rectify that condition. Sisera acknowledges the reversal that has taken place: it is he who is in want; it is Jael who is the mistress of his satisfaction. From the psychoanalytic point of view, the request is differentiated from the need, more passive and elementary, and from the desire, more active and ulterior. It stands between the two, as much in terms of activity as in the status of the subject. Intermediary, the request is always, according to Lacan (1966:814), a request for love. Poorly articulated, unconscious, it must accomplish that which is indispensable in the following stage, the constitution of the subject, capable of desire. According to the anthropological code, the request is here the intermediary form between silent obedience and the order that follows.

Sisera gets more than he asks for. Setting up the imminent misunderstanding produced by the double reversal of power relations, this excessive generosity disturbs the scheme of the request. Jael forces on Sisera the superposition of one ritual upon another. The request for love receives as its response the gift of love, but a different kind of love. The elementary love requested is maternal love. The love given is sexual. Jael skips two stages and imposes on her victim the stage of desire.

Before and after both the request and the offer, Jael covers Sisera with an object the identity of which is unknown. Sometimes it is translated as "rug" or "blanket," sometimes as "net." Baumgartner (1958:925) suggests that the word, unique in the Bible, be rendered as "curtain (which separates the woman's chamber [room] in the tents)." Of all the translations that I came upon, this one is the richest in meaning. It is found in one of the best-known dictionaries. Nevertheless, no one, to my knowledge, has chosen to adopt it. Such a meaning functions at several levels. According to the ethnographic code, it explains how Jael could have the object at her disposal. According to the ritualist code, it makes the object part of the rite of passage insofar as it emphasizes Sisera's separation from the exterior world. According to the gender code, it represents the suspension of limits between the sexes. On the one hand, by using it to cover Sisera, Jael deprives the curtain of its customary function, replacing it with another; the feminine domain is no longer separated from the rest of the tent. On the other hand, it remains contaminated by its original function, and Sisera, wrapped in this symbolic curtain, is integrated into and imprisoned within the feminine domain. Thus the answer "no [man]" that the former commander dictates receives its third meaning: he is not yet dead, but he is no longer a man.

Besides the meaning of the *word,* we can reflect on the meaning of the *act.* According to the thematic code, the act confirms the theme of sexuality; according to the anthropological code, it is part of the hospitality ritual and is intended to reassure; according to the underlying moral code, it reinforces an illusion of security and hence, reinforces deceit. According to the gender code, it signifies all these things at once: the act is sexual, tender, attentive, and ritual. The successive instances of that act should not necessarily be understood in the same light. For between them stands the act of excessive generosity that introduced the second ritual. This is why it can be said to confirm security the first time, (s)election the second. The configuration to cover (the infant)–to nurse–to cover (the sexual partner) is a crossroads of isotopies: maternity, the extreme consequence of the rite of passage, is doubled here, through the double sense of the word, by the sexual rite. It is not surprising that, as Boling puts it, Sisera allows himself to be both doped and duped. Thus he is excused.

How is this interpretation guided by the gender code? There are good reasons to suppose that it depends upon a masculine focalization. First, Sisera's perspective is presented here as the only perspective. He is the object and the addressee of the rituals. His safety, his life, and his salvation are at stake. His destiny will be accomplished. As for Jael, she fulfills like a priestess the functions that the three interwoven rituals assign her. Second, all three thematic lines introduced in the three verses 18–21 contribute to the strengthening of the central theme of annihilating shame. The fantasies implied in the ritualist interpretation—here the gender code is upheld by the anthropological code—wrap the theme of shame in a tissue of excuses, motivations, explanations. These are necessary to reassure the group that seems to be concerned here. It cannot be the "national" group itself, since Sisera is the enemy. The anxiety against which these reassuring explanations are directed can only be the anxiety common to Sisera's sexual class. At the dramatic level, they have the additional effect of delaying the catastrophe—*as the dream defers the awakening.* This dramatic effect rests on the tension provoked by the anxiety. Note in passing that this interpretation prescribed by the gender code joins the socially relevant criticism announced in the preface of the present study to an aesthetic appreciation of the text. Ideology and literary beauty are in no way mutually exclusive. Works of art have their roots in the society in which their creators live. The entanglement of biased interests, here gendered and nationalistic, with the formal elements of the literary work, has (en)gendered a text whose beauty can be valued even while the ideology implied in its images is challenged—as long as we do not separate these two aspects in order to bury one of them and forget it. They are naturally inseparable, so that dividing them by force would entail suppressions depriving followers on both sides of numerous possibilities, just as we have seen in the commentaries cited. In fact, the careful analysis of both aspects leads to their mutual illumination.

Third, this interpretion explains why the commentators cited throw themselves with such zeal upon the theme of deceived hospitality: in order to forget the theme of shame. They adopt this strategy because they are attuned to the masculine gender code, which they superimpose upon their personal, equally masculine code. If "Jael's treachery" is unforgivable, the shame of the men becomes forgivable. For the same reason, we imagine, Zakovitch was blind to the maternal aspect of the milk and the act of covering: "A good drink" and "a good lay" are much more edifying recreations for those who accept the ideologeme /honor-shame/ than are tenderness and security.

The Gender Code and the Song

In current editions of the Bible the song of Deborah *follows* the prose version. It is extremely difficult, for anyone accustomed to this reversal, to reestablish the perspective and to read the differences backwards. But more likely than not, this is how it happened: it is not the song that was censored with respect to the narrative. If there was censorship, it is certainly the narrative that was struck. Some details were removed, others were added, still others were modified. In point of fact, no hypothesis in this matter can be either proved or refuted. To avoid what would be futile discussion, I think it best to leave aside questions of influence. It is more important here to do justice to the differences in isolating what is specific to the song, without taking the comparative point of view as far as a position of opposition. I will try to start from the premise of a feminine gender code, which would explain the differences without relying on the necessity of a historical feminine subject (concerning which I, personally, have no doubts).

The song, in its lyric form and its incontestable oral base, is exceptional, as much in the book of Judges as in the Bible as a whole. I will try to integrate the results of the preceding chapters in interpreting the lyric form and orality from a gendered perspective. We have a good starting point in the research done in still-existent oral cultures. Katona (1979) established a relation between the division of cultural labor in the oral system and that between sexual groups. He observed that wherever these cultures still exist, the lyric genres are in the hands of the women, while the men practice the epic. In our case the hypothesis is confirmed. We should add, however, that the subgenres of the ode and the satire are not pure; they overlap. Obviously, this kind of classification cannot be projected upon an ancient text. The song of Deborah, however, has distinct characteristics of the ode and, to a lesser degree, of the satire. The ode to Yahweh is mimicked first by the ode to the tribes bound by allegiance and, then, by the ode to Jael, "blessed among women." The satire attacks the tribes not engaged in the holy war, and, further on, the Canaanite women. If these genres apply here, then the song is hybrid.

It is not in order to draw conclusions on the gender of the speaker that I cite Katona's article here. I am using it simply to show some of the problems that crop up when universal categories of this type are employed. When Katona enumerates the characteristics of the genres, straightaway a number of problems emerge (Table 2). The emphasis on village life does not mean that the women, like weathervanes, turn in all directions but are fixed in place. They, too, depart in search of adventure, but they also return to the village, in the end, to close the cycle traversed. The adventures of the men come to an end far from the village. As for the form, we have seen enough how far the epic form and, above all, narration in general go hand in hand with the historiographical project, an integral part, in turn, of the development of the patriarchal state. The style stripped bare of or enriched by details will have to be examined in the light of what has preceded.

These criteria are easy to misuse when the intimate relation between this classification of genres, even in its most simplified form, and the respective lifestyles of the two sexes, as predicated by the anthropological code, is ignored. If it is the men who depart in search of adventure, it is only logical that they choose those adventures as a theme; and if many things happen to them, it is only normal that they recount them. On the other hand, if in certain societies the women hardly leave the confines of their village, we can imagine that they do not have a great deal to recount from firsthand experience. What is more, they will not be motivated to identify with the adventurous heros. As for the details, there is no doubt a connection between the diversity of a life of adventures and the number of details that are retained, as there is between the monotony of a

Table 2

	Feminine Genres	Masculine Genres
Theme	Concentrated around the village and the family	Adventures outside
Form	Lyric	Epic
Style	Few details	Many details

relatively sequestered life and the absence of a "picturesque" imagination. Seen in this way, however, Katona's characteristics are already organized around a polemic opposition that I had promised myself to shun.

There are other ways to understand them. What happens, for instance, when we approach the song of Deborah through these categories? We will first have to clarify in what ways they are to be used. I will
apply them in the manner suggested by Gestalt psychology, whose application to narratological analysis was tested by Labov's school (1972).
The *form* provisionally adopted is then constituted by Katona's characteristics, the *figures* by the "deviations." Right away we notice that the
theme of the song would fall on the masculine side; Deborah's role as
judge, poetess, prophetess, and commander of the army shows how
much the accession of a woman to a different position influences the
orientation of her artistic production. On the other hand, the division of
literary *forms* between the sexes seems to be confirmed. We have seen
that, despite reservations about the projection of modern distinctions on
an ancient text, there is a style that can be defined as lyric and another as
narrative. The comparison of binary parallelisms with ternary structures
demonstrated that the difference between the two genres is clear. We
must not lose sight of the differences attributable to genre if we want to
avoid confusing the codes. That there is a relation between gender and
genre, and thus between gender code and literary code, is just as obvious.
While keeping these codes distinct, we will have to account for this relation.

Katona's third characteristic, the attitude toward details, warrants consideration. We have seen that the narrative adds details, and even entire
scenes. On the other hand, it also suppresses details. If Katona is right,
we can suppose that wherever the poetess gives more details than the
epic version, either the narrative has censored or the song considers
these details to be essential elements. The very notion of *detail* (Schor
1985) has to be reconsidered in this context. It presupposes a norm. A
detail is only considered as such from someone's point of view and relative to a particular notion of what is essential. This norm varies according
to the reader. "Detail" is defined as that which is small only when dimension is the criterion. Similarly, the "great turning points of action" often
described by the epic do not stand out as such unless fighting is regarded
as the principal theme. We can try to see what meaning the elements
admitted into the narrative of the song assume. For we can suppose that
these were considered "details" by the narrator of chapter 4.

The different categories of details are also worth examining. If Katona
refers to the factual and descriptive detail, the so-called picturesque detail, it is equally valid to apply this term to the *form* that these details take.
In order to grasp the meaning and the importance of these "details," a
comparison of the two versions, without any preconceived priority, can

again be revealing. The song offers a "surplus" at several points; we will concern ourselves with only a few examples from the crucial scene.

First, there is the praise of Jael; its specific meaning and the evolution of that meaning are studied in detail by Van Dijk-Hemmes (in preparation). Here, this praise is, most importantly, an explicit evaluation of Jael's act, something that is totally lacking in the narrative. Jael is praised in her capacity as woman, or, to be more precise, as woman in the tent. Next, in verse 25 there is "in a lordly bowl she brought forth cream," the climactic feature of a representation in ascending progression; here the new element "lordly bowl" draws our attention, especially in contrast with "the workmen's hammer." Finally, the details repeated in the representation of the act itself (second half of verse 26) and, above all, of Sisera's death, are remarkable. It is to them that those critics who condemn the tone of "savage delight" and "the gloating preservation of the gruesome details" (Cundall 1968:90) allude. After the scene of the murder itself, the evocation of Sisera's mother, which we have already considered, hardly looks like a detail. Yet it is missing from the narrative.

The narrative presented a series of masculine characters in cyclical movement, enemies but interchangeable in relation to the women. Sisera was the center, the mediator, and the principal actor in this cycle, all at once. In contrast, the episode of the murder in the song offers only a single character, the woman Jael. In the introduction of this character, her gender as much as her way of life is retained as significant:

> Blessed above [the] women be Jael,
> woman of Heber the Kenite
> blessed among [the] women in the tent.
>
> (5:24)

The complement "woman of Heber the Kenite" is often considered more recent (Boling 1975:114); despite the relevance this idea has for our present point of view, the lyric form prescribes that the tricolon be completed. Hence the decision to include it. The question is not without importance, seeing the enthusiastic commentaries that the proposition has inspired. The masculine gender code seems to incite certain critics (as, perhaps, the redactors of the book) to stress the dependency of Jael as spouse. Dhorme is one of those (1956:73); he notes regarding verse 4:11: "Le verset 11 est une parenthèse qui prépare *l'intervention de Héber* et de sa femme" (Verse 11 is a parenthesis which prepares *the intervention of Heber* and his wife) (my italics). As in the case of the unfortunate "Lappidoth" (4:4), it only requires a small step to make the woman into "the other half" of the man (and not the better one), who, then, would have taken charge of the enterprise himself. Whatever the case may be concerning this philological detail, the complement is here framed by two expressions that specify the gender of the character, "among (the) women." In the gendered interpretation of the narrative, I insisted on the significance of the presentation of Deborah as woman-prophetess for the reading of the sequence of the words. Here, the prophetic function is not thematized. This is not, however, because it gives way to the function of poetess. Quite the contrary: the second subsumes the first. In the world of the song in which poetry and history were still one and the same thing, there was no poetess that was not prophetess, proffering the just word. By analogy with this case, we had best take seriously the comparative complements attributed to Jael. That which she did, she did *as* a woman, a woman in the tent. In other words: as a person to whom a quite specific gendered social position was assigned.

Jael will be the thematic center of the brief lyric narrative that follows. She is the only character named in the stanza. Sisera is designated only as "he"; his name in verse 26 was added in the translation, and Dhorme comments (736): "Le nom de Sisera, mentionné au verset 20, n'est pas répété; on sait de qui il s'agit" (The name of Sisera, mentioned in verse 20, is not repeated; we know who it is). Grammatically speaking, Jael is the subject of all the verbs except "asked" and the verbs in verse 27. There is nothing here of the narrative version's dramatic episode describing Sisera's final attempt to reverse what is already his reversed role. Here Sisera becomes a character only at the very moment of his annihilation. Verse 25 includes, in ascending progression, a supplementary detail relative to the narrative: "in a lordly bowl she brought forth cream." Two elements are striking in the tricolon.

In the narrative, the water requested and the milk formed a contrast of simple opposition: the rudimentary chances of survival at the beginning versus the possibility of restoration. The opposition *survival–nourishment* signified *suspension of time–new beginning*, even while introducing the isotopy of maternity as hospitality taken to its extreme. Here, the initial opposition is turned into an ascending progression. In addition, the motif is not introduced by the hospitality ritual. The progression from water as minimum, via nourishing milk, to cream as luxurious delicacy, insists here on the honorific reception. The "lordly bowl" is the sign of the honor that falls to the man so magnificently received in the woman's tent. It is a great honor, it seems to say, to enter the universe of women: "in the tent." At the same time, the act, with the prior mention of the complement, has a certain ritual solemnity: the honor is that which falls to one condemned to death. It is important to understand that *honor* is here represented apart from its opposition to the *shame* from which it drew its meaning in the narrative. In the context of a reading guided by the feminine gender code, such an opposition, whose gendered ideological foundation we have seen, makes no sense.

If the "he," the anonymous masculine subject of the request, is treated nobly, it is also because he is the *other:* he is in women's territory, in the tent of this particular woman. Thus the contrast, doubly significant, between the lordly bowl and the workmen's hammer. The bowl is the sign of sovereignty. This sovereignty metonymically signifies the one who possesses and bestows it: the blessed woman. But she contaminates with her gesture of generosity the one who receives it. In the course of this transaction we can detect the intimations of another of its meanings. The guest is noble, not only because he is the addressee of the offer, but also because, as a guest and therefore by definition idle, he represents the class that opposes those who wield the workmen's hammer. As a former captain, he appears in all his nobility and is treated accordingly by her, but soon the other class will have its revenge. The workmen's hammer is the tool of the working world, of the quotidian world of active existence. In the case of nomadic tribes where the task of pitching the tent was the women's responsibility, it belonged to the feminine world. The feminine character is therefore depicted in the way she treats an intruder, a foreign element that has come transgressing the limit between two worlds (Lotman 1973:86). The theme of maternity that seems to be latent in the offering of the milk is certainly not emphasized here; whether or not it deserves to be activated is something we cannot resolve at this point.

The next verse presents Jael, the exemplary woman, at work. Plying the instruments of the working world that have been assigned to her by the organization of her society, she accomplishes, in fact, the ordinary gestures that are part of her work. She can do this because she acts as a member of the other group to which her feminine group belongs as well: she eliminates the enemy of her tribe. Here again, the gender code—mode of feminine life—is superimposed upon the anthropological code—mode of nomadic life—and upon the historical code—the Israelite war. All these codes without exception designate their own specific themes. All maintain the isotopy activated by the lordly bowl: the ritual and honorary suspension of the transgression of the limits between two worlds. Four themes are thus signified all at once in the single gesture celebrated four times: the lyric form makes it possible to recount "in detail"—differently, yes, but also far more effectively, than the epic.

One question has frequently been posed: how was Jael able to kill Sisera, standing upright and awake as he seems to be in this version? The question, inspired, it seems, by a concern for realism, was resolved by the author of the epic narrative in the manner we have seen: by swathing the blunder in explanatory excuses. Thus, "and he was fast asleep and he was weary and he died" (4:21). He offered no resistance because he was sleeping; he was sleeping because he had just made love and because he was drunk; he was drunk because he was gorged with soporific goat's milk or even wine, given by Jael; he could be led like a lamb to slaughter because Jael deceived him: we come full circle. The realist point of view is here distinctly colored by a gendered interest.

Provisionally overdetermined in this sense, we could add that the act is indeed hardly plausible. We could add that the peg was probably made of wood, in the bronze age and where the desert was never far, since the Israelites precisely lacked the iron chariots that Sisera boasted. Jael fights him on her territory, with her weapons: a wooden peg and a workmen's hammer. Let us try to imagine the act, executed on the temple of the man upright and awake, in step with the rhythm of the poetry, pounding, four strokes.

Was he really standing? The penetration of the hard instrument into the tender flesh, in pounding rhythm, is undoubtedly among the "details" that determined, without his knowing it, Zakovitch's thematic choice. It is tempting, indeed, to activate the latent sexual isotopy here. After the honor Jael awards him in qualifying herself, according to the ritual of matrimonial (s)election, as the (s)elected woman, this role reversal would retrospectively mark her act of generosity with irony. It would have sufficed if she gave *more* than water; by tripling the offer she gives a little too much.

Was he really standing? Could the detail of his position simply have been judged superfluous? No. For in the following verse, it is specified that he *fell*. Here is my answer: disregarding the realist criterion, the poetess portrays him as standing because it was necessary that he then fall. *To fall* is not only the passage from the upright to the prostrate position. It is the passage from the position of power of the respected commander to a position of annihilation, from life to death, and, according to the thematician, from sexual tension to postcoital release. The verb is repeated three times, and the last time, at the end of the ascending progression, the added "detail" gives the result that ensues: annihilation. Comparing this version to the other, we see how important it is to account for the codes that we use, and that the text may respect or disregard. It is only by the light of the later narrative that the song lacks verisimilitude here; alone, it has its own internal verisimilitude with respect to which the other has no relevance whatsoever.

But that is not all; given the above, we can take the image even further. He had to fall for still another reason: so that the thematic line latent in the motif of the *milk*, assuming its place now in a very different structure, could be reactivated. "Between her feet he collapsed, he fell": the formula is repeated. The "afterbirth" of Deut. 28:57, which, for Zakovitch, so irresistibly and exclusively suggests sexual pleasure, represents, in the context of Deuteronomy, the emblematic image of misery. More specifically, that image is the following: like the infant, the afterbirth will be *eaten by the woman from whom it issues*. If Zakovitch had taken the time to clarify the sexual content of each motif cited, I think he would have had difficulties here. On the other hand, the presence of the maternity theme in the image of the milk, if we accept it, is unquestionably determined by the powerful ironic contrast it establishes with this other, more terrible "nourishment," this image of the most complete annihilation possible: absolute regression.

The destruction of Sisera is not represented, here, in relation to his honor, his social position, his being as a man. It is represented in three successive steps that appeal to all the possible resources of the imagination of which a woman disposes: he falls, he ceases to live, he returns to the beginning of life to make a false start as afterbirth—we might say abortion: he never existed.

The imagination appealed to here can be illustrated by means of the concept of homonymy, which finds its pictorial equivalent in the celebrated example of the drawing representing simultaneously a rabbit and a duck. Both isotopies cannot be *seen* simultaneously, but it is possible to pass at will from one to the other. To gain a clearer understanding of the "homonymy" at work in the "central" scene of the song, compare a painting by Artemisia Gentileschi (Greer 1979), which, according to Zakovitch, represents a parallel case: the murder of Holofernes by Judith (see plates 1 and 2). On the whole, the work seems a bit confused: blood everywhere, scattered arms and legs, the woman divided in two. One can "read" this painting according to three isotopies concurrent in the song: murder, childbirth, and sexual intercourse, each of which mutually illuminates the others.

Is this to say that women are indeed sadistic monsters, whose savage imagination terrifies with good reason the gentle men who are its victims? In the interpretation of the narrative, I tried to refrain from judging in order better to analyze; I think it only fitting that I do the same here. However, in a society in which the women are "in the tent" and in which their position is utterly circumscribed, the number of moments when they have power over a man can be counted on the fingers of one hand. The confrontation of Jael with the enemy of her people unleashes in the mind the possibility of a reversal of roles. How to represent (to oneself) this (rare) situation in which a woman, for once, has absolute power over a man? It is important to see the image of 5:27 in this context: it is the liberation of an always limited imagination, as much in its experiences as in its means of expression. The images that are brought forth, liberated from the restrictions of the epic narrative, are metonymically inspired by the few experiences that this woman has by virtue of her own power: to mate, to give birth, and, now, to murder. Killing assumes the form of inverted sexual intercourse, of false childbirth. The exalted pleasure whose expression the lyric form authorizes is the pleasure of this power. Once the woman has been liberated by concern for the "national" good because Sisera is the enemy, the pleasure of

Plate 1.
The woman on the right is Judith; it is she who cuts off Holofernes' head. The second woman helps to hold the victim. In the paintings of the period (seventeenth century) in which a similar theme is represented, a second woman, young servant or old procuress, is often added. See both Rembrandt's and Rubens' *Samson and Delilah*. (Artemisia Gentileschi, "Giudetta e Oloferne," reproduced by permission of the Galleria degli Uffizi, Firenze.)

Plate 2

1. Axis of childbirth: the arms of the victim are "homonymous" with the thighs of the mother.
2. Axis of the murder: the second woman seems to accomplish the act.
3. Axis of sexual intercourse: the first woman pushes away her lover with her hands at the moment of orgasm.

subverting the roles within her own assigned space, where the privacy of the woman is guaranteed, prevails over every other consideration, every other pleasure.

Brought back to the confirmed order of things by the image of the victim's mother, the inspired poetess does not relent so soon. She passes quickly from the woman in the tent to those sequestered in the splendid but equally imprisoning palace. Sisera's mother happens to be a bad mother, whatever sense we choose to ascribe to this concept. She is not even capable of knowing what has happened to her son. Ignorant after the fact, she is the negative image of the prophetess, who understands in anticipation. She is not only a bad mother; she is also a bad woman. "One womb/girl, two wombs/girls for each hero's head"—in such terms she evokes the contrary of what has really happened. She uses the crude word "womb" for /woman/. One woman/two women for each hero's head? She does not know how truly she speaks. One woman, Jael, coming to the aid of another, Deborah, was enough for the head of the false hero taking flight full speed into the feminine domain.

The crude term "womb" suggests the inverted, ironic view of the preceding scene as I have interpreted it. It was not sufficient that one or two women put to death, striking at his head, a single man; it was also necessary that, taking literally the crude language of the other woman, she/they be inspired by her/their function as "womb." Organ of childbirth and intercourse, the womb, figurative in the vulgar *gendered* expression whose usage is analogous to that of the French word "nana" (girl),* literally serves as instrument of murder, by means of the sexual attraction that draws Sisera within reach. The woman who borrows masculine language to designate other women as wombs richly deserves such a lesson. And she receives it in a most appropriate form: the gift of false prophetic discourse, retrospective but ambiguous. Without even knowing it, Sisera's mother utters the "right word." It is true that her son has received riches—milk, cream, the lordly bowl—for the tender part of his head. The head of the hero has its vulnerable point, designated either as the neck, where the head can be severed, or as the temple, where it can be pierced, as in a reversed rape. It is the Achilles' heel of domination and rational censorship. One womb, two wombs, and the hero falls.

---

*"Nana" is the word used familiarly in French, mostly by men, to refer to a young woman, usually as possession or object of attraction of a man. In certain contexts, "girl" is a rough equivalent in English, as in "How was the party? Any girls?"—TRANS.

CONCLUSION

Semiotics, difference, criticism, trans-, multi-, or interdisciplinarity: the key terms of the discussion pursued in this study will have to be reconsidered now if this book is to live up to its intention. The first and last terms of the series have been in fashion so long that they are in danger of losing all precision, and, therefore, all significance.

The semiotic perspective is often the target of the accusation of imperialism; nothing, after all, eludes the production of meaning, and hence nothing eludes semiotic analysis. The stars in the heavens, the cars on the highways, the roar of planes, anything can be integrated within semiotics provided only that we desire it. Even so, there lies the limit, the limit indispensable to knowledge. *We,* that is to say, the whole cultural community influenced by the Bible, have urgently desired that the biblical texts, whatever their origin may be, have meaning. The consequences of this desire are staggering: we know the enormous impact of mythologies, religions, and ideologies on our daily life, on the course of history, on a culture that chooses to orient itself by a body of texts. The attribution of meaning to those texts happens globally and implicitly, and, depending on the culture's subgroups and their interests, the meanings are different and more or less elusive. Too many presuppositions obviously taken for granted prove, when we take a closer look, to be poorly, or incompletely, or differently adopted by one group or another. Semiotic uncertainty is the very basis of the existence of academic practice. If we could always determine what texts signify, in the case of the Bible we would have performed the task long ago and filed away the results. There would be nothing more to say about it.

Texts by definition being semiotic constructs, necessitating the active participation of readers or listeners for their existence, the textual object is dynamic, unstable, elusive. To study it, we cannot be content with merely analyzing the text; it is, after all, the attribution of meaning that constitutes it. But to analyze how others attribute meaning is to interpret; and rather than suppress the interpretive act, the semiotician must embrace it. It is for this reason, in opposition to the meta-semioticians who abjure interpretation because it will always be uncertain and biased, that I allowed myself the pleasure and the freedom to practice it in the preceding chapters. To refuse to interpret is in the final analysis a non-semiotic attitude. It is naïve to believe that we can analyze without interpreting, that we can work and live without lending meaning to the world around us.

The discussion that constitutes this book was based on the presupposition that the academic practice of the university inevitably has its semiotic aspect, which is not the only important aspect—there lies one of the misunderstandings that lead to the accusation of imperialism—but one that all disciplines share. Here, then, is a first stake in interdisciplinarity. I tried to bring out, in the practice of four representative disciplines that demonstrate the problematics involved in the interpretation of ancient texts, what disciplines have in common. All without exception function through the attribution of meaning. The concept of code was introduced, not to suggest the existence of pseudomathematical rules, of ineluctable laws, but to show that the implicit character of diverse presuppositions can make us *believe* in those ineluctable laws; to show that a code is whatever we choose to give the status of a code. All that "goes without saying" because we no longer think about it determines the interpretations that we believe to be "inscribed in the text." How, for example, can one seriously maintain that in Judges, chapter 4, Jael is praised for her act? We have seen this happen, nevertheless. It happens when the critic believes it "goes without saying" that chapters 4 and 5 are merely two versions of the same real and indubitable event. It is only too easy to criticize "errors" of this kind. But the omission, the absence of any consideration of the gender of the poet of chapter 5, is that an "error" too? No; each critic is free to declare certain questions significant at the expense of others. This is one of the rules of the game: the semiotic perspective has taught us that there are no limits to the semiotic act; thus, it is impossible to be, or even to try to be, complete.

Given the semiotic aspect inherent in every disciplinary procedure, the analysis of a number of examples of disciplinary practice from the perspective of the attribution of meaning (on the basis of codes dictated by disciplines), is an enterprise that can be qualified as *multidisciplinary*. Such an enterprise declares the concepts that constitute the program of a theory applicable to several disciplines. It is the most widespread view of semiotics; it applies everywhere. It is not yet an interdisciplinary procedure because the theory has yet to be integrated by disciplines themselves. It is, we might say, imported: brought in from the outside. And it is also, as I practiced it, critical. I tried to distinguish disciplinary codes in the true sense from the implicit codes—moral, religious, aesthetic—that go unnoticed, smuggled in like contraband. This differentiation contributed to the analysis of the text as a dynamic object, since the meanings assigned were not separated from the text taken in isolation. Already at this rudimentary level, the two senses of the term "criticism" went hand in hand: the differentiation of the codes helped to sort out the ethnocentric prejudice, among others, from the understanding of ancient codes, as fragile and biased as it may be.

Codes that cross the boundaries of different disciplines unimpeded and without being excluded from the academic community have been qualified as *transdisciplinary*. These are the familiar codes we have long known without ever understanding their specific character. Tradition claims that it is the literary critic who thematizes thematics; the other disciplines simply practice it. Thematics thus *crosses* disciplines. It can do this with so little resistance because its unifying principle exerts an almost irresistible attraction. This in turn proceeds from the profoundly centripetal tendency of cultural communities still in expansion, while, underground, subcultures develop because the opposing centrifugal movement is just as inevitable. Hence the dynamics of cultural life that no power ever manages to eliminate. Thematics may well have the advantage of transdisciplinarity on its side; still, the basic principle that makes it so easy to accept it at the same time constitutes its conservatism. It is thematics that, in diverse forms—mythology, for example—secures for those anguished by change and for those who seek after absolute, transhistorical truth the reassuring illusion that certain things "have always been like that." It is thus illusion that makes us believe, even today, that the patriarchal structures of modern society are inevitable because eternal. The thematics that unifies the two versions of Jael's disturbing act contributes to this illusion. The theologian who claims at the expense of the obvious pantheism of the text that Yahweh is practically absent from the song of Deborah unifies similarly, but in more subtle fashion. Under the pretext of a historical perspective, differential by definition, he represents the theology of the song as a "primitive" state of the Yahwist theology that attains its perfection later. Evolutionism is thus no less unifying. Far from being truly historical, it acknowledges but one single acceptable state: the present, that to which all previous stages have led in a straight line, and at which we have now arrived. It is the most antihistorical of attitudes.

The transdisciplinary perspective is necessary if we are to liberate ourselves from the restrictions—valuable to a certain point—of disciplines. Unifying, it precludes the incorporation of disciplinary results. Here is where the *interdisciplinary* attitude intervenes. This means consciously and specifically appealing to diverse disciplines when there are good reasons for it. A very clear case was the insertion of the ideologeme /honor-shame/ implicated by the anthropological code. That ideologeme can emerge only in a society where the division of labor between the sexes is strict. It would make no sense whatsoever where both sexes participate in the military domain. At a simpler level, the interpretation of the murder weapon as tied to the feminine world *at the epoch* appealed to the anthropological and historical codes. They were indispensable. Taken in isolation, each would have been insufficient. A literary analysis that ignored the particular theology of the song would be a poor one; disregarding the situation of orality, it would be unable to account for the deictic structure of the text. No discipline operating alone could possibly account for the impact of the text. For these authors lived in a community they shared with their listeners/readers, one that was not limited by any discipline; and it is their semiotic acts that constitute the object.

Contrary to the unifying principle of an innocently transdisciplinary thematics, an interdisciplinary analysis in which each appeal to a discipline is specifically motivated is by definition differential. This is why the *critical* dimension is enriched. The example of Dhorme, who attributed an interest in colored cloths to the feminine sex, reminding us of the missionaries of the good old days who gave colored beads to the blacks in exchange for their souls, demonstrated to what point the ignorance of other disciplines leads: at best, to stupidity; at worst, to ethnocentric arrogance.

I did not attempt to give a representative view of disciplines and approaches. I wanted to limit the discussion to disciplinary procedures seen as codes, that is, as rules of correlation between expression and content. It is a perspective rather than a strictly defined method, a philosophical process rather than a search for certainty. The analyses were limited to a number of aspects at the expense of others certainly just as important. This was because my goal was simpler. On the one hand, I wanted to show not only to what extent codes are institutionally anchored but also how they are biased by group interests outside of recognizable institutions; on the other hand, I wanted to propose an interdisciplinary hermeneutics that would not scorn interpretation. Such an approach, while being disciplined, takes a differentiated reaction to texts that interest us—in spite of or by virtue of their differences—further than disciplinary interpretations. The concept of code, flexible when necessary, more tightly delineated when it was profitable, proved to be useful as a critical approach. Criticizing the current hermeneutic practice, it helps us to *differentiate,* undermining the cultural homogenization that impoverishes our dominant culture as much as its subcultures.

REFERENCES

Ackerman, James S. 1975. "Prophecy and Warfare in Early Israel: A Study of the Deborah-Barak Story." *Basor* 220: 5–15.

Ackroyd, P. R. 1952. "The Composition of the Song of Deborah." *Vetus Testamentum* 2: 160–62.

Albright, W. F. 1968. *Yahweh and the Gods of Canaan: A Historical Analysis of Two Contrasting Faiths*. London: The Athlone Press.

Allen, Christine Garside. 1979. "On Me Be the Curse, My Son!" In *Encounter with the Text. Form and History in the Hebrew Bible*, edited by Martin J. Buss, 159–72. Philadelphia: Fortress Press/Missoula: Scholars Press.

Alonso Schökel, Luis. 1965. *The Inspired Word: Scripture in the Light of Language and Literature*. New York: Herder.

Alt, A. 1967 (1925). "The Settlement of the Israelites in Palestine." In *Essays on Old Testament History and Religion*. Garden City, N.Y.: Doubleday. ("Die Landnahme der Israeliten in Palästina." In *Kleine Schriften zur Geschichte des Volkes Israel*, 89–125. München: C. H. Beck, 1953.)

Alter, Robert. 1981. *The Art of Biblical Narrative*. New York: Basic Books.

Auld, Graeme A. 1984. *Joshua, Judges and Ruth*. The Daily Study Bible. Edinburgh: The Saint Andrew Press.

Bal, Mieke. 1981a. "Notes on Narrative Embedding." *Poetics Today* 2, 2: 41–60.

———. 1981b. "The Laughing Mice, or on Focalization." *Poetics Today* 2, 2: 203–12.

———. 1982. "Mimesis and Genre Theory in Aristotle's Poetics." *Poetics Today* 3, 1: 171–80.

———. 1984a (1977). *Narratologie*. Utrecht: Hes Publishers.

———. 1984b. "Introduction." *Psychopoetics-Theory*, Special issue of *Poetics* 13, 4/5: 279–300. (Also in *Psychopoetics at Work*, Special issue of *Style*.)

———. 1985. *Narratology: An Introduction to the Theory of Narrative*. Toronto: University of Toronto Press.

———. 1986. *Femmes imaginaires. L'Ancien Testament au risque d'une narratologie critique*. Utrecht: Hes / Montréal: HMH / Paris: Nizet.

———. 1987. *Lethal Love: Feminist Literary Readings of Biblical Love Stories*. Bloomington: Indiana University Press.

Barstad, Hans M. 1984. *The Religious Polemics of Amos. Supplements to Vetus Testamentum* 34. Leiden: Brill.

Barthes, Roland. 1966. "L'effet du réel." *Communications* 4.

Baumgartner, Walter. 1958. *Lexicon in Veteris Testament Libros*. Leiden: Brill.

Bäuml, Franz H. 1986. "Medieval Texts and the Two Theories of Oral-Formulaic Composition: A Proposal for a Third Theory." *New Literary History* 16, 2: 32–49.

Benveniste, Emile. 1966. "L'homme dans la langue." In *Problèmes de linguistique générale*, 1, 225–88. Paris: Gallimard.

Berlin, Adele. 1985. *The Dynamics of Biblical Parallelism*. Bloomington: Indiana University Press.

Blenkinsopp, J. 1961. "Ballad Style and Psalm Style in the Song of Deborah—A Discussion." *Biblica* 42: 61–76.

Boling, Robert G. 1975. *Judges. A New Translation with Introduction and Commentary*. Anchor Bible, vol. 6A. Garden City, N.Y.: Doubleday.

Boon, James A. 1982. *Other Tribes, Other Scribes. Symbolic Anthropology in the Comparative Study of Cultures, Histories, Religions and Texts*. Cambridge: Cambridge University Press.

Booth, Wayne C. 1961. *The Rhetoric of Fiction*. Chicago: University of Chicago Press.

Bourdieu, Pierre. 1979. *La Distinction: Critique sociale du jugement*. Paris: Editions de Minuit.

Bowra, Cecil M. 1961. *Heroic Poetry*. London: Macmillan.

———. 1963. *Primitive Song*. New York: Pathfinders Press.

Buss, Martin J. 1979. "Understanding Communication." In *Encounter with the Text. Form and History in the Hebrew Bible*, edited by Martin J. Buss, 3–44. Philadelphia: Fortress Press / Missoula: Scholars Press.

Chaney, Marvin. 1976. "HDL-II and the "Song of Deborah": Textual Philological and Sociological Studies in Judges 5, with Special Reference to the Verbal Occurrences of HDL in Biblical Hebrew." Ph.D. diss., Harvard University.

Cohen, A., ed. 1980. *Joshua. Judges*. Hebrew Text and English Translation, with Introductions and Commentary. Soncino Books of the Bible. London, Jerusalem, New York: The Soncino Press. (Herein Slotki's commentary.)

Coogan, M. D. 1978. "A Structural Analysis of the Song of Deborah." *The Catholic Bible Quarterly* 40: 132–66.

Craigie, P. C. 1969. "The Song of Deborah and the Epic of Tukulti-Ninurta." *Journal of Biblical Literature* 88: 253–60.

———. 1972. "A Reconsideration of Shamgar Ben Anath (Judg. 3:31 and 5:6)." *Journal of Biblical Literature* 91: 239–41.

———. 1977. "Three Ugaritic Notes on the Song of Deborah." *Journal for the Study of the Old Testament* 2: 33–49.

———. 1978. "Deborah and Anath: A Study of Poetic Imagery." *Zeitschrift für die Alttestamentliche Wissenschaft* 90: 374–81.

Culley, Robert C. 1967. *Oral-Formulaic Language in the Biblical Psalms*. Toronto: University of Toronto Press.

———. 1976. *Studies in the Structure of Hebrew Narrative*. Philadelphia: Fortress Press.

Cundall, Arthur E., B.A., B.D. 1968. *Judges. An Introduction and Commentary*. Tyndale Old Testament Commentaries. Leicester: Inter-Varsity Press.

Dhorme, Edouard. 1956. *La Bible. Ancien Testament*. Paris: Gallimard, Editions de la Pléiade.

Dijk-Hemmes, Fokkelien van. 1983. "Een moeder in Israel." In *Wending* 9: 688–95.

———. In prep. "Blessed Be among the Women."

Dolezel, Lubomír. In press. *Chapters from the History of Structural Poetics*.

Drinker, Sophie. 1977. *Music and Women. The Story of Women in their Relation to Music*. New York: Zenger.

Dudley, Edward, and Maximillian E. Novak, eds. 1972. *The Wild Man Within*. Pittsburgh: University of Pittsburgh Press.

Dupont-Roc, Roselyne, and Jean Lallot. 1980. *Aristote—la poétique*. Paris: Editions du Seuil.

Eco, Umberto. 1976. *A Theory of Semiotics*. Bloomington: Indiana University Press.

———. 1984. *Semiotics and the Philosophy of Language*. Bloomington: Indiana University Press.

Fabian, Johannes. 1983. *Time and the Other. How Anthropology Makes Its Object*. New York: Columbia University Press.

Fensham, F. C. 1964. "Did a Treaty between the Israelites and the Kenites Exist?" *Bulletin of the American Schools of Oriental Research* 175: 51–54.

Finley, Sir Moses. 1977. *The World of Odysseus*. London: Chatto and Windus.

Finnegan, Ruth. 1977. *Oral Poetry, Its Nature, Significance and Social Context*. Cambridge: Cambridge University Press.

Fokkelman, J. 1981. *King David. Narrative Art and Poetry in the Books of Samuel*, vol. 1. Assen: Van Gorcum.

Foley, John Miles. 1977. "The Traditional Oral Audience." *Balkan Studies* 18: 145–53.

Freedman, David Noel. 1975. "Early Israelite History in the Light of Early Israelite Poetry." In *Unity and Diversity: Essays in the History, Literature and Religion of the Ancient Near East*, edited by H. Groedicke and J. J. M. Roberts, 3–35. Baltimore: Johns Hopkins University Press.

———. 1976. "Divine Names and Titles in Early Hebrew Poetry." In *Magnalia Dei*, edited by F. M. Cross et al., 55–107. New York: Doubleday.

———. 1977. "Pottery, Poetry, and Prophecy: An Essay on Biblical Poetry." *Journal of Biblical Literature* 96: 5–26.

———. 1979. "Early Israelite Poetry and Historical Reconstructions." *Symposia:* 85–96.

Garbini, Giovanni. 1978. "**Parzōn* 'iron' in the Song of Deborah?" *Journal of Semitic Studies* 23: 23–24.

Geertz, Clifford. 1966. "Religion as a Cultural System." In *Anthropological Approaches to the Study of Religion*, edited by M. Bantom. London: Tavistock.

———. 1983 (1974). "'From the Native's Point of View': On the Nature of Anthropological Understanding." In *The Pleasures of Anthropology*, edited by Morris Freilich. New York: New American Library. (Original: *Bulletin of the American Academy of Arts and Sciences* 28:1).

Genette, Gérard. 1972a. "Métonymie chez Proust." In *Figures III*, 41–66. Paris: Editions du Seuil.

———. 1972b. "Fréquence." In *Figures III*. Paris: Editions du Seuil.

———. 1976. *Mimologiques*. Paris: Editions du Seuil.

Gerleman, G. 1951. "The Song of Deborah in the Light of Stylistics." *Vetus Testamentum* 1: 168–80.

Geus, C. H. J. de. 1976. *The Tribes of Israel: An Investigation into Some of the Presuppositions of Martin Noth's Amphictyony Hypothesis*. Assen/Amsterdam: Van Gorcum.

Gillie, R. C., and James Reid. 1924. *The Bible for Youth*. London: T. C. & E. C. Jack Ltd.

Globe, A. 1974. "The Literary Structure and Unity of the Song of Deborah." *Journal of Biblical Literature* 93: 493–512.

Gooding, D. W. 1982. "The Composition of the Book of Judges." *Eretz Israel* 16: 70–79.

Goody, Jack, and Ian Watt. 1968. "The Consequence of Literacy." In *Literacy in Traditional Societies*, edited by Jack Goody, 27–84. Cambridge: Cambridge University Press.

Gore, Charles, Henry Leighton Goudge, Alfred Guillaume, eds. 1928. *A New*

Commentary on Holy Scripture. London: Society for Promoting Christian Knowledge.

Gottwald, Norman K. 1979. "Sociological Method in the Study of Ancient Israel." In *Encounter with the Text. Form and History in the Hebrew Bible,* edited by Martin J. Buss. Philadelphia: Fortress Press / Missoula: Scholars Press.

Greer, Germaine. 1979. *The Obstacle Race.* London: Secker & Warburg.

Greimas, A. J. 1970. *Du sens. Essais sémiotiques.* Paris: Editions du Seuil.

Greimas, Algirdas Julien, and J. Courtès. 1979. *Sémiotique. Dictionnaire raisonné de la théorie du langage.* Paris: Hachette.

Grice, H. P. 1976. "Logic and Conversation." In *Syntax and Semantics,* vol. 3, edited by R. Cole and J. L. Morgan. New York: Academic Press.

Griffin, Jasper. 1980. *Homer on Life and Death.* Oxford: Blackwell.

Habermas, Jürgen. 1968. *Erkenntniss und Interesse.* Frankfurt am Main: Suhrkamp.

Hauser, Alan J. 1980. "Judges 5: Parataxis in Hebrew Poetry." *Journal of Biblical Literature* 99/1: 23–41.

Havelock, A. 1963. *Preface to Plato.* Cambridge: Cambridge University Press.

Honigmann, John J. 1963. *Understanding Culture.* New York: Harper & Row.

Iser, Wolfgang. 1974. *The Implied Reader: Patterns of Communication in Prose Fiction from Bunyan to Beckett.* Baltimore: Johns Hopkins University Press.

Jakobson, Roman. 1971. "On Linguistic Aspects of Translation." In *Selected Writings,* 2. The Hague: Mouton.

Jameson, Fredric. 1981. *The Political Unconscious. Narrative as a Socially Symbolic Act.* London: Methuen.

Johnson, Barbara. 1980. *The Critical Difference.* Baltimore: Johns Hopkins University Press.

Katona, Imre. 1979. "Reminiscences of Primitive Divisions of Labor between Sexes and Age-groups in the Peasant Folklore of Modern Times." In *Toward a Marxist Anthropology,* edited by S. Diamond, 377–83. The Hague: Mouton.

Keil, C. F. and F. Delitzsch. 1980. *Commentary on the Old Testament in Ten Volumes.* vol. II. Joshua, Ruth, I & II Samuel. Grand Rapids, Michigan: William B. Eerdmans Publishing Company.

Kloos, Peter. 1981. *Culturele antropologie.* Assen: Van Gorcum.

Korsten, Frans-Willem. 1985. "Brunhildes voorbeeld." In *Ik zing mijn lied voor al wie met gaat. Vrouwen in de volksliteratuur,* edited by Ria Lemaire, 183–96. Utrecht: Hes mÿ Publishers.

Kristeva, Julia. 1968. "Poésie et négativité." *L'Homme* 2 (viii): 36–63.

———. 1974. *La révolution du langage poétique.* Paris: Editions du Seuil.

Kugel, James L. 1981. *The Idea of Biblical Poetry. Parallelism and Its History.* New Haven: Yale University Press.

Labov, William. 1972. *Explorations in Semantic Theory.* The Hague: Mouton.

Lacan, Jacques. 1966. *Ecrits.* Paris: Editions de Seuil.

Lapointe, Roger. 1977. "Tradition and Language: The Import of Oral Expression." In *Tradition and Theology in the Old Testament,* edited by Douglas A. Knight, 125–42. Philadelphia: Fortress Press.

Leach, Edmund. 1983. "Why did Moses Have a Sister?" In Edmund Leach and Alan Aykock, *The Structuralist Interpretation of Biblical Myth.* Cambridge: Cambridge University Press.

Lemaire, T. 1984. "Antropologie en schrift—aanzetten tot een ideologiekritiek van het schrift." In *Antropologie en ideologie,* edited by T. Lemaire. Groningen: Konstapel.

Lind, Millard C. 1980. *Yahweh is a Warrior. The Theology of Warfare in Ancient Israel.* Scottdale, Pennsylvania/Kitchener, Ontario: Herald Press.

Lindars, B. 1979. "The Israelite Tribes in Judges." *Supplements to Vetus Testamentum* 30, 95–112. Leiden: Brill.

Lord, A. 1960. *The Singer of Tales.* Cambridge, Mass.: Harvard University Press.

Lotman, Jurij. 1973. *La structure du texte artistique.* Paris: Gallimard.

McKenzie, J. L. 1967. *The World of the Judges.*

Malamat, Abraham. 1979. "Israelite Conduct of War in the Conquest of Canaan." *Symposia* I: 35–56.

Martin, J. D. 1979. "The Office of Judge in Pre-Monarchic Israel." Glasgow, *Oriental Society Transactions* 26: 64–79.

Mayes, A. D. H. 1969. "The Historical Context of the Battle against Sisera." *Vetus Testamentum* 19: 353–60.

——. 1974. *Israel in the Period of the Judges.* Studies in Biblical Theology, Second Series 29. London: SCM Press.

——. 1977. "The Period of the Judges and the Rise of the Monarchy." In *Israelite and Judaean History,* edited by John H. Hayes and J. Maxwell Miller. London: SCM Press.

——. 1983. "Deuteronomistic Editing of *Judges.*" In *The Story of Israel between Settlement and Exile. A Redactional Study of the Deuteronomic History,* 58–80. London: SCM Press.

Miller, J. Maxwell. 1976. *The Old Testament and the Historian.* Philadelphia: Fortress Press.

——. 1977. "The Israelite Occupation of Canaan." In *Israelite and Judaean History,* edited by John H. Hayes and J. Maxwell Miller, 213–84.

Moore, G. F. 1984 (1895). *A Critical and Exegetical Commentary on Judges.* International Critical Commentary. Edinburgh: T. & T. Clark.

Moser, Walter. 1981. "Translating Discourse: Inter-Discursive Mobility in the Early Romantic Encyclopedia." *The Eighteenth Century. Theory and Interpretation* 22, 1: 3–20.

Müller, Hans Peter. 1966. "Aufbau des Deboraliedes." *Vetus Testamentum* 16: 446–59. Leiden: Brill.

Murray, D. F. 1979. "Narrative Structure and Technique in the Deborah-Barak Story (Judges IV:4–22)." *Supplement to Vetus Testamentum* 30: 155–89.

Nathhorst, B. 1970. *Formal or Structural Studies of Traditional Tales.* Stockholm.

Neil, William. 1975. *Harper's Bible Commentary.* New York/London: Harper & Row.

Nielsen, Eduard. 1954. *Oral Tradition. A Modern Problem in Old Testament.* London: SCM Press.

Noth, Martin. 1930. *Das System der Zwölf Stämme Israels.* Beiträge zur Wissenschaft vom Alten und Neuen Testament IV, 1.

Ong, Walter. 1977. *Interfaces of the Word. Studies in the Evolution of Consciousness and Culture.* New York/Ithaca: Cornell University Press.

——. 1982. *Orality and Literacy. The Technologizing of the Word.* London: Methuen.

——. 1984. "Orality, Literacy and Medieval Textualization." *New Literary History* XVI, 2:1–12.

Patrick, Dale. 1979. "Political Exegesis." In *Encounter with the Text. Form and History in the Hebrew Bible,* edited by Martin J. Buss, 139–52. Philadelphia: Fortress Press/Missoula: Scholars Press.

Pelc, Jerzy. 1971. "On the Concept of Narration." *Semiotica* 3: 1–19.

Pelto, Pertti J. 1970. *Anthropological Research. The Structure of Inquiry.* New York: Harper & Row.

Pitt-Rivers, Julian. 1976. *The Fate of Shechem and the Politics of Sex.* Cambridge: Cambridge University Press.

Polzin, Robert. 1980. *Moses and the Deuteronomist.* New York: Seabury Press.

Rad, G. von. 1962, 1965. *Old Testament Theology.* 2 vols. Translated by D. M. G. Stalker. New York: Harper & Row.

Richter, Wolfgang. 1963. *Traditionsgeschichtliche Untersuchungen zum Richterbuch.* Bonner Biblische Beiträge 18. Bonn: Peter Hanstein Verlag GmbH.

———. 1964. *Die Bearbeitung des 'Retterbuches' in der deuteronomistische Epoche.* Bonner Biblische Beiträge 21. Bonn: Peter Hanstein Verlag GmbH.

———. 1971. *Exegese als Literaturwissenschaft. Entwurf einer alttestamentlichen Literaturtheorie und Methodologie.* Göttingen: Vandenhoeck & Ruprecht.

Ricoeur, Paul. 1984. *The Role of Metaphor. Multidisciplinary Studies of the Creation of Meaning in Language.* Toronto: University of Toronto Press.

Rose, Jacqueline. 1984. *The Case of Peter Pan, or the Impossibility of Children's Fiction.* London: Macmillan.

Sahlins, Marshall. 1968. *Tribesmen.* Englewood Cliffs, N.J.: Prentice Hall.

Saïd, Edward, 1978. *Orientalism.* New York: Vintage Books.

La Sainte Bible. 1961. Traduite en français sous la direction de l'école biblique de Jérusalem. Paris: Editions du Cerf.

Saussure, Ferdinand de. 1967. *Cours de linguistique générale.* Edited by Rudolf Engler. Wiesbaden: Harrassowitz.

Scheub, Harold. 1975. "Oral Narrative Process and the Use of Models." *New Literary History* 6: 352–77.

Schogt, Henry G. 1984. *Sémantique synchronique: synonymie, homonymie, polysémie.* Toronto: University of Toronto Press.

Schor, Naomi. 1985. *Breaking the Chain. Feminism, Theory and French Realist Fiction.* New York: Columbia University Press.

Schunck, K. D. 1966. "Die Richter Israels und ihr Amt." *Supplements to Vetus Testamentum* 15: 252–62.

Soggin, J. Alberto. 1981. *Judges. A Commentary.* London: SCM Press.

Stein, Dominique. 1980. "Une lecture psychanalytique de la Bible est-elle possible?" *Concilium Variis Linguis* 158: 39–50.

Sternberg, Meir. 1984. "The Bible's Art of Persuasion: Ideology, Rhetoric, and Poetics in Saul's Fall." *Hebrew Union College Annual* LIV (1983): 45–82.

Stock, Brian. 1983. *The Implications of Literacy: Written Language and Models of Interpretation in the Eleventh and Twelfth Centuries.* Princeton: Princeton University Press.

Suleiman, Susan. 1987. "Nadja, Dora, Lol V. Stein." In *Discourse in Psychoanalysis and Literature,* edited by Shlomith Rimmon Kenan. London: Methuen.

Tedlock, Dennis. 1981. *Phonography and the Problem of Time in Oral Narrative Events.* Urbino: Documents du centre international de sémiotique.

Todorov, Tzvetan. 1981. *Mikhaïl Bakhtine. Le principe dialogique.* Paris: Editions du Seuil.

Trible, Phyllis. 1976. *God and the Rhetoric of Sexuality.* Philadelphia: Fortress Press.

———. 1984. *Texts of Terror.* Philadelphia: Fortress Press.

Tsevat, Matitiahu. 1975. "Common Sense and Hypothesis in Old Testament Study." *Supplements to Vetus Testamentum.* Congress Volume, XXVIII, 217–30. Leiden: Brill.

Turner, Victor. 1974. *Dramas, Fields and Metaphors.* Ithaca: Cornell University Press.

———. 1980. *The Ritual Process. Structure and Anti-Structure.* Ithaca: Cornell University Press.

Weippert, Manfred. 1971. *The Settlement of the Israelite Tribes in Palestine.* Studies in Biblical Theology, Second Series 21. London: SCM Press.

———. 1972. "'Heiliger Krieg' in Israel und Assyrien: Kritische Anmerkungen zu Gerhard von Rads Konzept des 'Heiligen Krieges' im alten Israel." *Zeitschrift für die Alttestamentliche Wissenschaft* 84: 460–93.

———. 1979. "The Israelite 'Conquest' and the Evidence from Transjordan." In *Symposia Celebrating the Seventy-Fifth Anniversary of the Founding of the American Schools of Oriental Research (1900–1975)*, edited by Frank Moore Cross. Cambridge, Mass.: American Schools of Oriental Research.

Weiser, A. 1959. "Das Deboralied—eine gattungs- und traditionsgeschichtliche Studie." *Zeitschrift für die Alttestamentliche Wissenschaft* 71: 67–97.

White, Hayden. 1972. "The Forms of Wildness: Archeology of an Idea." In *The Wild Man Within*, edited by Edward Dudley and Maxmillian E. Novak, 3–38. Pittsburgh: University of Pittsburgh Press.

Willis, John T. 1979. "Redaction Criticism and Historical Reconstruction." In *Encounter with the Text. Form and History in the Hebrew Bible*, edited by Martin J. Buss, 84–89. Philadelphia: Fortress Press/Missoula: Scholars Press.

Yacobi, Tamar. 1982. "Fictional Reliability as a Communicative Problem." *Poetics Today* 2, 2: 113–26.

Yadin, Yigael. 1979. "The Transition from a Semi-Nomadic to a Sedentary Society in the Twelfth Century B.C.E." *Symposia:* 57–68.

Zakovitch, Yair. 1981. "Sisseras Tod." *Zeitschrift für die Alttestamentliche Wissenschaft* 93, 3: 364–74.

Zumthor, Paul, 1982. *Introduction à la poésie orale.* Paris: Editions du Seuil.

———. 1984. "The Text and the Voice." *New Literary History* 16, 2: 66–92.

INDEX